Amsterdam

Dan Colwell

CITYSCAPE

JPMGUIDES

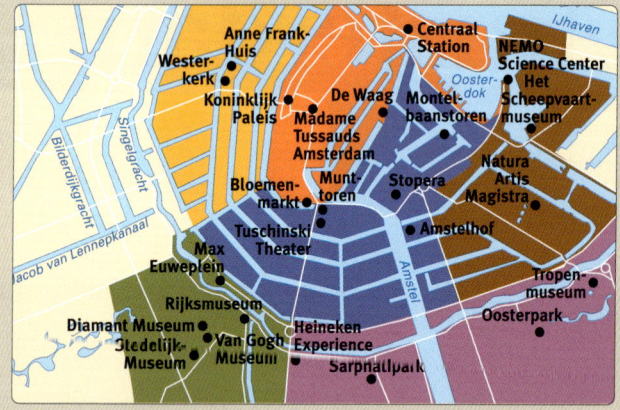

Amsterdam's centre is surprisingly small, and you will soon get used to the layout of its horse-shoe canals. You can nip quickly across bridges to reach its core in a few minutes, or zigzag lazily along the banks beneath the trees, drinking in the reflections of the tall houses in the water. To make sightseeing easier we have split the city into manageable sections, coded by colour.

Contents

Features

Water Web	8
Bricks and Mortar	16
Shopping Streets	24
Café Culture	38
In the Marketplace	48
For the Children	56
Dutch Masters	66
Curiosity Shops	72

Maps

Amsterdam region	106
Utrecht	107
Delft	108
The Hague	109
Rotterdam	110

Fold-out Map

Amsterdam
Tram network

Symbols

★ Our favourites
M Metro
T Tram
B Bus

cityLights 5
cityPast 11
citySights 19
    Central Amsterdam 20
    Jordaan and
    Western Grachtengordel 32
    Southern Grachtengordel and
    the Amstel 40
    Plantagebuurt and Docklands ... 50
    Museumbuurt and Leidseplein .. 58
    De Pijp and Oosterparkbuurt 68
    Excursions 74
cityBites 83
cityNights 91
cityFacts 97
Index 111

cityLights

At first glance, the city seems to confirm all the images by which we know it. Amsterdam really is full of elegant canals, quaint bridges and old coffee houses. Trams and bicycles continually whizz through the streets. Tulip fields and windmills are only a stone's throw away, and although Amsterdammers have given up clogs for Nikes these days, you'll find they remain as welcoming as if their city were the friendly village it sometimes resembles.

But the picture is more complex. Because of its tradition of openness and tolerance, Amsterdam is also a cosmopolitan mix of cultures. This began as far back as the 17th century, when Spanish Jews and French Huguenots came here to escape from persecution. Today, new Amsterdammers include modern-day refugees from Africa and Asia, people from former Dutch colonies such as Surinam and Indonesia, and those who have flocked here since the 1960s, attracted by Amsterdam's famously relaxed social attitudes. If you look again closely at those famous canals, you'll find that their waters reflect a variety of faces, and a living, changing city.

A YEAR OF CULTURE

Virtually all Dutch museums charge an entrance fee. If you're planning to visit several museums in Amsterdam or further afield, it is worth investing in a Museumkaart. For €39.95 (€19.95 for those aged 18 and under), plus a once-only joining fee of €4.95, it gives a year's unlimited access to over 400 different museums in the Netherlands, of which 33 are in Amsterdam. You can buy one at the ticket counter in the participating museums or obtain one online, www.museumkaart.nl.

The Best Ingredients

One result of the cultural melting-pot is that a city of only 700,000 people can vie with the world's biggest for offering the visitor a tempting array of international cuisine, live music, cinema, night life, performing arts and art galleries. Here you will find the best rijsttafel outside Indonesia, some of the liveliest discos and jazz bars in Europe, and the greatest collection of van Goghs in the world—not forgetting, of course, such cultural marvels as the prestigious Concertgebouw for classical music, and the incomparable Rijksmuseum, with its magnificent array of Dutch Masters. Add to this the spice of the infamous red-light district, and you have the recipe for an experience that will captivate all tastes.

Double Dutch

A cousin of English through its German roots, the Dutch language will surprise you with the familiarity of some of its words. However, the way they are

pronounced is guaranteed to baffle. Luckily, Amsterdam is an international city in anyone's language, and its inhabitants have developed a remarkable multilingual talent. They may well appreciate it if you try to speak a few words of Dutch, but they won't be so merciless as to let you go on very long before breaking out in perfect English, German or, like as not, good French, Spanish or Italian. One thing you can be sure of is that there'll be no problem communicating.

Points of View

Amsterdammers are all in love with their city, and who can blame them? Before long, you may start feeling the same way. You can admire it from many angles. Get a bird's-eye view from the top of the Westerkerk or the Beurs van Berlage, or a duck's perspective as you float leisurely along on a canal boat. If you're in a more energetic mood, follow the locals and watch it flash past above the handlebars of a bicycle. Alternatively, you can always let it come to you, while you spend just 20 minutes more sitting outside that cosy café in the Jordaan.

But whether you view it as a 17th-century gem or a 20th-century melting-pot, a museum piece or bastion of modern liberal values, Amsterdam is a city that will never fail to surprise every time you return to take another look.

WATER WEB

It's no wonder that Amsterdam is famous for its canals: there are over 160 of them stretching in total for more than 75 km. The big four—Singel, Herengracht, Keizersgracht and Prinsengracht—are known collectively as the Grachtengordel, or Canal Belt (*gracht* being the Dutch word for canal) and fan out concentrically from the centre of the city like the strands of a spider's web. The easiest way to see the canals is by boat, but if you want to linger over a particularly fine 17th-century mansion or spend some time deciding for yourself which exactly is the smallest house in Amsterdam, nothing beats strolling along the elegant streets beside them. Bear in mind that house numbers start at the Brouwersgracht side of the city across from Jordaan.

The Big Four

Not to be confused with Singelgracht, which is further out, **Singel** is part of the original defensive moat that sat in front of a wall surrounding inner Amsterdam in the 15th century. A few reminders of this can still be seen, such as the Munttoren, whose base was part of a city gate dating from 1490, and the Oude Leliestraat bridge, which once bore a lookout tower. Take a closer look at the bridge just above the waterline and you'll see what was a small prison used in medieval times for locking up rowdy drunks.

At the dawn of the 17th century, Europe's most dynamic economic powerhouse was still like a small village. It didn't stay that way for long. In 1607 the first commission was given to expand the city beyond the Singel with the construction of three new canals—they were dug by hand by the thousands of refugees who had flooded into Amsterdam from towns in southern Holland still under Spanish control.

Herengracht (Gentlemen's Canal) was the first and the grandest, as the fabulously wealthy merchants of the Golden Age built themselves a Millionaire's Row like no other. Between Leidsestraat and Vijzelstraat is the prized Golden Bend section, which contains the finest of the mansions.

The second of the new canals was the **Keizersgracht**, named in honour of the Holy Roman Emperor Maximilian I, but noticeably less grand than the Herengracht. **Prinsengracht**, or the Prince's Canal, a nod to

William the Silent, Prince of Orange, benefits from bordering the Jordaan area to the west, thus taking on some of that district's livelier atmosphere rather than the solemnity of its more stately neighbours.

Radial canals

If the Big Four are like the main strands of the web, the smaller, radial canals that link them are the ones that actually hold the thing together. And whereas the grand townhouses and mansions of the main canals were built for the rich merchant class and are now occupied by museums and multinational companies, the narrow buildings of the **Brouwersgracht**, **Leidsegracht** and **Reguliersgracht** were once inhabited by artisans and workers and are now home to some of Amsterdam's loveliest cafés and intriguing speciality shops. There were originally more of these charming radial canals, however: Rozengracht, Leidsestraat, Elandsgracht and Vijzelstraat were filled in at the start of the motor age to provide more space for traffic.

Keeping things clean

Given that so much of the city is occupied by canals, you might be forgiven for wondering whether it is in effect sitting in a huge pool of stagnant water and how smelly this makes it. Fortunately, the Golden Age architects of the 17th century were clever enough to build in a network of sluice gates: the large ones on the Amstel date from 1674 and allow fresh water to enter the canals while pumping out the less salubrious water four times a week, making the Grachtengordel a treat for the nose as well as the eyes.

cityPast

Vincent van Go...
Wheatfield wi...

Beginnings
It seems fairly certain that until the 13th century, the site now occupied by Amsterdam was nothing but a watery marshland. However, the location at the mouth of the Amstel and the IJ, an inland arm of the former Zuider Zee, was perfect for fishing, and a small village was established. To protect themselves from floods, the inhabitants built dikes on either side of the Amstel, and in about 1270 the first dam was constructed between the dikes—the Amsteldam.

Medieval Centre

Just five years later, the ruling Count of Holland, Floris V, granted the people of the town exemption from tolls. Amsterdam rapidly developed into a city of merchants, trading as far away as the Baltic.

In 1345, the town received a financial boost from the unlikeliest of events. A dying man was given last communion but he couldn't swallow the communion bread. When the regurgitated host was thrown onto the fire, it refused to burn. The incident was declared to be a miracle, and Amsterdam became a popular destination for pilgrims for the next two centuries.

Fortified City

The Counts of Holland left Amsterdam more or less to get on with things, but in 1419 Duke Philip the Good of Burgundy became Count of Flanders and subsequently extended his influence throughout the region. In fact, the resulting political stability consolidated Amsterdam's growing wealth and importance.

During the 1420s, the Singel canal was dug as a protective moat, and defensive walls were erected. However, in the last quarter of the century, possession of Holland passed through marriage to the Habsburgs, and thus began a troubled era of rule under Catholic Spain.

Spanish Netherlands

The country found itself a neglected part of the vast Habsburg Empire. Charles V assumed control in 1515 and abdicated in favour of his son, Philip II of Spain in 1555. Whereas Protestantism had been spreading in cities like Amsterdam, Philip was famous for his strict Catholicism, and the clash between the two brought the Netherlands out of the Habsburg backwater. There were major anti-Catholic riots and uprisings in 1566, put down ruthlessly the following year by the Duke of Alva and 10,000 Spanish troops. In 1568, William of Orange emerged as the nationalist leader of the Dutch Revolt, and although total victory over the Spanish wasn't secured for many years, by 1578 the Alteration had occurred in Amsterdam, when municipal power passed from Catholics to Protestants. With the influx of Antwerp's merchants after the Spanish attack of 1585, and the weakening of Spanish naval power following the defeat of the Armada in 1588, the stage was set for a Golden Age.

Golden Age

Holland's Golden Age was one of the most remarkable flowerings of national and cultural self-confidence the world has ever seen. It can virtually be dated from the foundation of the Dutch East India Company in 1602. Dutch merchants had been exploring the Far East since the 1590s, and their successful voyages enriched Amsterdam beyond all expectations. On the back of this boom, Hendrick de Keyser's churches and towers dignified the Amsterdam skyline, the building of the Herengracht, Keizersgracht and Prinsengracht transformed the city on the ground, and Dutch artists such as Rembrandt made Amsterdam the centre of 17th-century European art.

During this time, the Dutch Navy fought off the English and the French, and figures such as Admiral Michiel de Ruyter became national heroes by ensuring Holland's position as a leading world power.

Decline and Fall

The bubble burst with the rise of larger, more aggressive neighbours in the 18th century. London surpassed Amsterdam as the premier financial centre. The steam ran out of the Netherlands

Landmark church towers: the Westerkerk and the Zuiderkerk. ▶

great surge, as it came once again under foreign sway, claimed by the French and the Austrians. In the 1790s, further trouble struck when Dutch republicans sided with invading French Revolutionary troops, and William V fled to England. Following the accession of Napoleon, it briefly became the Kingdom of the Netherlands under the emperor's brother, Louis Bonaparte, until Napoleon dismissed him in 1810 and absorbed the country into the French Empire. The Netherlands was at its lowest ebb.

An Independent Kingdom

The modern nation came into being in 1813, as Napoleon lost his grip on Europe and William of Orange returned to be proclaimed King. The next century saw the gradual development of Holland's social welfare system, with slum clearance, the advent of trade unionism for the diamond workers, and pioneering work in birth control and women's rights.

AMSTERDAMSE BOS

The vast Amsterdams Forest, a few kilometres southwest of the city centre, was created from unused turf- and wetlands in the 1930s to keep the unemployed occupied, as well as to provide a fine woodland for city dwellers to enjoy. It includes the Bosbaan, a stretch of water for boating, a tree-climbing park, cycle routes and planned walks, slopes for winter sports, a goat farm where you can buy cheese, playgrounds for children, an open-air theatre and the Molshoop visitor centre, which will teach you more about the unusual history of the area. The Visitor Centre is open daily noon–5pm, though the Bos itself never closes. You can get there by taking bus 170 or 172 from Centraal Station.

The Netherlands remained neutral during World War I, although food became scarce. In 1932 the Afsluitdijk separating the Zuider Zee from the North Sea was completed, and the lake formed behind the dike named the IJsselmeer. The danger of being a small nation with big neighbours was once again seen in 1940, when Germany refused to recognize Dutch neutrality and invaded.

Rebuilding a Nation

World War II was traumatic for the Netherlands. The country had been devastated and the Jewish population almost destroyed. However, the city had shown remarkable resilience. The dockworkers' strike of February 1941 in protest at the transportation of Jews is a justly celebrated event. In 1946 Queen Wilhelmina granted Amsterdammers the right to put the words Heldhaftig, Vastberaden, Barmhartig—Heroic, Resolute, Merciful—on the city's coat-of-arms in recognition of their courage during the German occupation.

After the war, Holland transformed itself into a modern social democracy. It off-loaded its colonial possessions, initiated a welfare state, and became a keen member of the European Community. But Amsterdam sometimes seems to have gone its own way. Since the 1960s, its reputation as the capital of European counter-culture has firmly established itself. But in a way, this is only further evidence that modern Amsterdam is still as tolerant, democratic and self-confident as it was in its golden heyday 300 years ago.

The three St Andrew's Crosses come from the city's coat of arms.

BRICKS AND MORTAR

The very existence of the city is a triumph of builders over the power of the water. But it was a hard-won victory. Few of the earliest buildings remain—they were made of wood, as brick and stone were too heavy for the soft soil. Even then, many of them simply sank into the marsh; the rest burned down in the great fires of the 1420s. A rare survivor is the wooden house at Begijnhof 34, dating from 1470. The oldest building in Amsterdam, however, is the Gothic Oude Kerk, built with foundations solid enough to have lasted since the early 1300s.

City of brick...

By the 16th century, architects had begun to work out that in Amsterdam you need to drive a building's foundation posts a long way down if you want to prevent it subsiding—in fact, the most solid layer of sandy soil is 50 m below the surface. Once this technological breakthrough was made, builders started using brick with gusto, and the city rapidly took on its current appearance—though some buildings still slump alarmingly to one side. You'll notice that a lot of them also tilt forward. That's intentional, and designed to stop the furniture that's hauled up via the gable winch-hook from bumping into the front of the building. The staircases inside are just too small for furniture-moving.

The city's skyline is still characterized today by the graceful, ornamented spires and towers designed by Amsterdam's most important Golden Age architect, Hendrick de Keyser (1565–1621). His strikingly decorative Zuiderkerk spire, the lantern tower added to the Munttoren and the spectacular Westerkerk are landmark structures that represent the pinnacle of Italian-influenced Dutch Renaissance style.

De Keyser's immediate successors were more influenced by the stricter architectural proportions of neoclassicism. You won't find many oriental-looking spires bursting from the pilasters, pediments and columns of the Trippenhuis, completed in 1664 by Justus Vingboons (1620–98), or the undoubtedly grand Stadhuis (now the Royal Palace), designed in 1648 by Jacob van Campen (1595–1657).

...and of gables

The highpoint of Amsterdam's architectural achievement is the extraordinary assemblage of 17th- and 18th-century houses along the principal canals. This individualistic, bourgeois architectural form almost represents the distilled essence of Dutch culture and character. Though the canals are graced by everything from tiny houses as narrow as their own front door to rococo Louis XV-style mansions, in general the size and structure of the buildings share a basic architectural blueprint. The marvel of Amsterdam is that there is such little uniformity in their actual appearance. This is due to individual flourishes such as carved pediments and idiosyncratic sculptural details on the façade, but it is most appealingly achieved by the variety of gables to be seen. These are purely decorative features that conceal the roof and assert the individuality of the house owner. There are four main versions to look out for. The plain spout-gable was originally used on wooden buildings but carried on into the Renaissance era; the step-gable, resembling a series of steps on either side of the gable, was popular in the first half of the 17th century; this gave way to the cleaner lines of the neck-gable, which architects found more appropriate for the mid-17th-century interest in Roman-style pediments and flat cornices; and finally, the bell-gable, a fancy baroque form that reached its zenith in the 18th century.

The Amsterdam School

Many brick buildings in the city date from the time of the Amsterdam School, a style of architecture that was popular from 1910 to 1930 and whose major proponents were Michel de Klerk, Johan van der Mey and Piet Kramer, all of whom worked for Eduard Cuypers before 1910. The constructions are characterized by round shapes and the use of art glass, wrought ironwork and windows with horizontal bars. One of de Klerk's designs, a former post office, now houses the Amsterdamse School Museum Het Schip devoted to the movement, which is related to Expressionism (open daily except Mon, 11am–5pm, Spaarndammerplantsoen 140, near Westerpark, ◘ 22). The building's shape recalled a grand cruise liner, and like Renzo Piano's NEMO, with green, pre-oxidized copper sheets resembling a prow, is a reminder of the city's relationship with the sea.

citySights

Central Amsterdam	20
The heart of town	
Jordaan and Western Grachtengordel	32
Lots of atmosphere beside the canals	
Southern Grachtengordel and the Amstel	40
Gracious living, entertainment district,	
and the old Jewish quarter	
Plantagebuurt and Docklands	50
History, science and modern architecture	
Museumbuurt and Leidseplein	58
Art and culture	
De Pijp and Oosterparkbuurt	68
A lively and colourful shopping district	
Excursions	74
From grand old cities beside the sea	
to tulip plantations	

CENTRAL AMSTERDAM

Until the 17th century, central Amsterdam was enclosed by city walls and a defensive moat, now the Singel canal. The area on the east side of the Dam is known locally as de Walletjes (for its location within the walls), though is more notorious as Amsterdam's red-light district, centred on the oldest part of the city. Most of the windows here are now occupied by young clothes designers, although the area still flaunts a little of its old business without a hint of shame, as you will see from the rows of sex cinemas, porn bookshops, and ladies in various states of undress staring out from their window seats. The area has some of the finest old buildings in Amsterdam, not least the Oude Kerk and the Museum Ons Lieve Heer op Solder, both on Oudezijds Voorburgwal.

THE DISTRICT AT A GLANCE

SIGHTS

Architecture
Centraal Station 20
Beurs van Berlage ★.21
Nieuwe Kerk 22
Koninklijk Paleis 22
Begijnhof 26
Dutch East India Building..........27
Zuiderkerk ★..........27
Waag..................27

Oude Kerk ★............28
Sint Nicolaaskerk......28
Schreierstoren 29

Atmosphere
Dam Square 22

Browsing
De Bijenkorf 23
Magna Plaza..........23

Memorial
Nationaal Monument..............22

Museums
Madame Tussauds Amsterdam 23
Amsterdam Museum ★ 23
Allard Pierson Museum 27
Museum Ons' Lieve Heer op Solder ★ 28

WALKING TOUR 30

WINING AND DINING 84

Centraal Station (F1) Looking every inch a palace to rival the one in Dam Square, the neo-Renaissance Centraal Station, designed by P.J.H. Cuypers, was opened in 1885 and gives a spectacular introduction to the city. Initially criticized for blocking the view of the port, it is now a main focal point for the city.

Centraal Station is the hub of the transport network.

Virtually all the trams stop here; tourist and travel information offices are just outside and most of the canal boat trips start nearby. **M Centraal Station or T 1, 2, 4, 5, 9, 13, 16, 17, 24, 25, 26**

Beurs van Berlage (E2) South along Damrak from Centraal Station, this magnificent modernist stock exchange, designed by H.P. Berlage, was begun in the late 19th century, although it wasn't opened until 1903; its staggering 9 million bricks had been so heavy that immediate subsidence made it too dangerous for use. Particularly eye-catching are the Commodities Exchange Room and the Chamber of Commerce Meeting Hall, where the key to Berlage's success can be seen in the exquisite detail, and a place of commerce is raised to a work of art. It has two concert halls and is also used for temporary exhibitions and congresses. • Café open Mon–Sat 10am–7pm, Sun 11am–7pm • Guided tours: to book ☎ 020 530 41 41 • 12 Damrak 277 **M Centraal Station or T 1, 2, 4, 5, 9, 13, 14, 16, 24, 25**

Dam Square (D2). Dam Square is the place where 13th century herring fishermen built the first dam across the Amstel River, giving the city its name. It has remained the symbolic heart of Amsterdam ever since. At different times, it has been used for public executions, Republican rallies and protests against cruise missiles. Several important buildings and monuments cluster here (the Royal Palace, the Nieuwe Kerk, the Nationaal Monument), and it's the place where younger travellers hang out in summer. ☎ 1, 2, 4, 5, 9, 13, 14, 16, 17, 24, 25

Nationaal Monument (E3) The simple white obelisk commemorates those who died between 1940–45; the 12 urns behind the monument contain soil from eleven Dutch provinces and from Indonesia. ☎ 1, 2, 4, 5, 9, 13, 14, 16, 17, 24, 25

Nieuwe Kerk (D2) Slightly shouldered into a corner of the Dam by the Royal Palace, the Nieuwe Kerk was here long before the palace was even thought of. Built at the beginning of the 15th century (it's only the "new" church in relation to the even older Oude Kerk), it was damaged by several fires culminating in the Great Fire of 1645, which destroyed the interior. The carved pulpit and Jacob van Campen's ornate organ house date from just after this time. The church is the Dutch equivalent of Westminster Abbey. Great figures of the past are buried inside, such as Admiral Michiel de Ruyter and the national poet, Joost van den Vondel. Since 1814 Dutch monarchs have been invested in this church, the last one being Queen Beatrix in 1980. • **Daily 10am–5pm, Thurs till 9pm during exhibitions** • To book guided tours ☎ 020 626 81 68 or rondleidingen@nieuwekerk.nl ☎ 1, 2, 4, 5, 9, 13, 14, 16, 17, 24, 25

Koninklijk Paleis (D2) The Royal Palace was formerly a grandiose town hall, designed by Jacob van Campen in the mid-17th century in Palladian style and intended to demonstrate the power and wealth of the city's burgomasters during the Golden Age. The building was converted into a palace in 1808 when Napoleon's brother, Louis Bonaparte, was briefly set up as King of the Netherlands and took a fancy to it. The interior is decorated with works by Dutch Masters, such as Ferdinand Bol and Govert Flinck. • **Daily noon–5pm; closed during royal events** ☎ 020 620 40 60 or www.koninklijk huis.nl ☎ 1, 2, 4, 5, 9, 13, 14, 16, 17, 24, 25

CENTRAL AMSTERDAM 23

De Bijenkorf (E2) The Grande Dame of Amsterdam's big stores faces the Royal Palace. There's a good range of quality clothes, shoes, jewellery and houseware, and when it gets too much you can cool down at the 2nd floor restaurant, La Ruche, with a fine view over Dam Square. • Mon 11am–7pm; Tues, Wed 10am–7pm; Thurs, Fri 10am–9pm, Sat 9.30am–7pm, Sun 11am–7pm • Dam 1 ☎ 1, 2, 4, 5, 9, 13, 14, 16, 17, 24, 25

Madame Tussauds Amsterdam (D3) Well-known waxworks depicting the famous and infamous, with many historical Dutch figures thrown in for good measure, as well as sound, lights and special effects. • Daily 10am–6.30pm, July and August 10am–8.30pm ☎ 020 522 10 10 • Peek and Cloppenburg Building, Dam 20 ☎ 1, 2, 4, 5, 9, 16, 24, 25

Magna Plaza (D2) The former GPO has been converted into a rather civilized shopping mall. Behind the Royal Palace, the Plaza has five floors of fashion boutiques and a good café on the second floor. • Mon 11am–7pm; Tues–Sat 10am–7pm (Thurs till 9pm); Sun and holidays noon–7pm; closed Dec 25, 26, Jan 1, Apr 30 • Nieuwezijds Voorburgwal 182 ☎ 1, 2, 5, 13, 14, 17

Amsterdam Museum (D3) Entered from bustling Kalverstraat, which runs south from Dam, via a peaceful courtyard, and occupying a restored 16th-century orphanage, this first-rate historical museum covers the development of the city from the 13th century onwards. There is an interesting room devoted to the orphanage itself, as well as displays which include armour, weaponry, paintings, audio-visual programmes, a carillon you can play yourself, and archaeological finds. Inevitably, much attention is given to the Golden Age and the Dutch East India Company. A few of the paintings are particularly noteworthy. Rembrandt's gruesome *Anatomy Lesson of Dr Jan Deijman* should not be missed, and Cornelis Anthonisz's overview of Amsterdam, painted in 1538, is the oldest-known plan of the city. Be sure to look at the Civic Guard Gallery (Schuttersgalerij), an arcade adorned with huge canvasses from the 16th and 17th centuries commissioned by the good men of the guard, who were clearly rather pleased with themselves. It is part of the museum but serves as a public thoroughfare during the day and has free admission. • Mon–Fri 10am–5pm, Sat–Sun 11am–5pm ☎ 020 523 18 22 • Kalverstraat 92 ☎ 1, 2, 4, 5, 9, 14, 16, 24, 25

SHOPPING STREETS

Almost everyone who visits Amsterdam—and most of the locals too—end up walking along **Kalverstraat** at some point. This long shopping precinct goes from the Dam all the way to Munttoren and contains a variety of department stores, souvenir shops, cheap clothes shops and an assortment of familiar high street names such as H&M at 125, Waterstone's at 152 and the American Book Center at Spui 12. At the top near Muntplein, in the shiny Kalvertoren Shopping Centre (entered on Singel 457), you can shop at the Vroom & Dreesmann department store and take the lift to the top for a panoramic view from the café. Going south from Kalverstraat you come to **Leidsestraat**, which has an array of fine clothes shops that are not excessively expensive, besides brand stores such as Littala and Ace Juweliers. The luxury department store Metz & Co at Nos. 34–36, founded in 1740, has had the right to call itself "Purveyor to the Royal Family" since 1849. There's a restaurant beneath the dome.

Running two streets west of the Museum Quarter, **P.C. Hooftstraat** is the place for haute couture and designer clothing. You won't find many bargains here, though that's hardly surprising given that you will find boutiques like Tourbillon, Zegna, Vuitton, Chanel and Cartier. On P.C. Hooftstraat you can be sure that the atmosphere is restrained, the cuts stylish, and you'll discover what the affluent Amsterdam woman about town will be wearing this season.

In and around **Nieuwe Spiegelstraat** and **Spiegelgracht**, running from the Herengracht to the Rijksmuseum, is Amsterdam's main art and antique dealing area. You may find works by up-and-coming artists or some by painters from Amsterdam's Golden Age in the 17th century, but even if they are all beyond your budget it is perfectly acceptable to look around without buying.

9 Straatjes is a fun shopping area between Rozengracht and Leidsegracht. The name refers to the nine streets running between the four big canals. Here you'll find fascinating small shops selling goods ranging from designer fashion to hip vintage clothing, creative books, natural cosmetics or unusual kitchen utensils and gadgets. The Witte Tandenwinkel (White Teeth shop) is at Runstraat 5, perfect if you feel guilty about succumbing to the smell of the delicious chocolates sold just around the corner at the Chocolaterie Pompadour, Huidenstraat 12.

Between Rembrandtplein and Frederiksplein, **Utrechtsestraat** has not only a number of very good clothes and shoe stores but also some great places for browsing. At No. 52, Concerto is an Amsterdam institution. Here you'll find everything you can think of in music, on CD or vinyl and from Indie pop to jazz or classical music. At Nos. 110–112, A La Carte conveys you all around the world in maps and travel books. Take a break from shopping in one of the many restaurants and cafés, such as Café Oosterling, an old brown café near Frederiksplein.

Haarlemmerstraat is a small but lively shopping street running from the Singel near Centraal Station to the Haarlemmerpoort. Among the many restaurants and cafés you'll find all kinds of shops ranging from a vitamin store, a skateshop, design and vintage clothing boutiques to Het Grote Avontuur at No. 25, which sells interior items, gifts and bric-a-brac from all over the world, everything with a fair trade label. To rest your feet, make your way to the the superb Art Deco cinema The Movies at Haarlemmerdijk 161–163, to watch an art film or dine in its restaurant.

Begijnhof (D3) One of Amsterdam's discreet charms is its *hofjes*, attractive little courtyards hidden behind rows of houses. Located just south of the Amsterdam Museum, the Begijnhof is an outstanding example. Founded in 1346 by the Beguine sisterhood, it remains a haven of peace for visitors and residents alike. Het Houten Huys, the wooden building at No. 34, dates from the 1470s and claims to be the oldest house in Amsterdam. Look inside Nos. 30–31, where you will find a hidden church from the time of the Alteration, when Protestants took control of the city and Catholics had to hold their services behind closed doors. In the centre of the *hof* is the Engelse Kerk, built at the end of the 14th century but handed over in 1607 to the English Reformed Church, whose members had moved to Holland to avoid persecution. The pulpit panels

HIDDEN HOFJES

The best-known *hofje*, or secluded courtyard, in Amsterdam is the Begijnhof, established in the 14th century by the Beguines, a group of lay nuns who voluntarily withdrew from the world outside. But the majority of them are in Jordaan and were built as almshouses for the elderly in the 17th- and 18th centuries. To this day they present a calmer, quieter face to visitors and a momentary retreat from the city's hue and cry. Ones to look out for include **Claes Claesz Hofje** (Eerste Egelantiersdwarsstraat 3), which dates from 1616 and is now colonized by students of the Amsterdam Conservatory; **St Andrieshofje** (Egelantiersgracht 107–145), founded in 1617 through the donation of a rich cattle farmer called Gerritszoon; and **Lindenhofje** (Lindengracht 94–112), the oldest, built in 1614.

were added by the 20th-century De Stijl artist, Piet Mondrian. • **Daily 9am–5pm** • **Nieuwezijds Voorburgwal 373** 🚋 1, 2, 4, 5, 9, 14, 16, 24, 25

Allard Pierson Museum (E4) A 5-minute walk from the Begijnhof on the other side of Rokin, the museum is home to Amsterdam University's archaeological collection, begun in 1934. Intriguing artefacts include an Iranian libation vessel in the shape of a ram, Egyptian mummies and bronze statues, olive oil flasks and urns from Ancient Greece, and a huge Roman Dionysian sarcophagus decorated with elaborate sculptures. • **Tues–Fri 10am–5pm, Sat–Sun 1–5pm** ☎ 020 525 25 56 • **Oude Turfmarkt 127** 🚋 4, 9, 14, 16, 24, 25

Dutch East India Building (E3) It is almost impossible to visit Amsterdam without being aware of the company that gave the city its great wealth in the 17th century and the architecture and art that developed as a result. This huge structure, occupying a substantial chunk of Kloveniersburgwal, was the nerve centre of an operation that extended throughout the world. The outside of the building (Verenigde Oost-Indische Compagnie Gebouw) is fairly dull these days—it is used as part of the university—but the splendid Dutch Renaissance courtyard is simply dazzling. • **Oude Hoogstraat 24** Ⓜ Nieuwmarkt

Zuiderkerk (E3) Across Kloveniersburgwal, the South Church, built by Hendrick de Keyser in 1603 with a tower dated eleven years later, is now used for exhibitions. Beautifully located among the narrow streets of the old town, it was greatly admired by Christopher Wren, and its influence can be seen on many of the English architect's own masterpieces in London. The church—along with its West, East and North cousins – is what was known as a "compass church", a landmark building by which people could navigate their way around the city—and given Amsterdam's low level skyline and de Keyser's distinctive spires they can still function that way for confused tourists. • **Mon–Fri 10am–5pm, Sat by appointment** ☎ 088 010 2280 • **Zuiderkerkhof 72** Ⓜ Nieuwmarkt

Waag (E3) When the Waag, due north of the Zuiderkerk, was built in 1488 it was a city gate. Since then, the town has never quite known what to do with the Gothic, seven-turreted oddity. It has been a weigh-house, a trade hall for various guilds, a museum, and is now a restaurant and creative centre. During the 17th century, the surgeons' guild's anatomy lectures were held here. Rembrandt was invited to attend on two occasions and the result was a famous pair of paintings, one of which, *The Anatomy Lesson of Dr Jan Deijman*, can now be seen at the Amsterdam Museum. • Nieuwmarkt 4 Ⓜ Nieuwmarkt

Oude Kerk (E2) In the heart of the red-light area, set back from the Oudezijds Voorburgwal canal, the oldest parish church in the city might just occasionally induce more spiritual thoughts in the minds of its wayward parishioners as they go about their business. Built in the 14th century and the oldest structure in the city, this venerable Gothic church has seen many changes, not least when its own treasures were cleared out after the Protestant reformation. The interior still looks bare, but has some fine 16th- and 17th-century stained glass windows, an attractive marble screen by van Campen, and a monumental Christian Vater organ of 1724. Beneath the small choir organ on the north side is the tomb of Rembrandt's wife, simply inscribed "Saskia". • Mon–Sat 11am–5pm, Sun 1–5pm ☎ 020 625 82 84 • Oudekerksplein 23 🚋 4, 9, 16, 24, 25

Museum Ons' Lieve Heer op Solder (Museum Amstelkring) (F2) This small museum is well worth seeking out. Inside the building, a gem from Amsterdam's Golden Age, you might be forgiven for thinking you've walked into a painting by Vermeer. Refurbished by its merchant owner, Jan Hartman, in the early 1660s, the house has remained virtually unchanged ever since, and the beautifully decorated rooms encapsulate the age. At the top of the house is the remarkable "Attic Church", built as a result of the prohibition of open Catholic worship. Furnished in Flemish baroque, and with an altar painting by Jacob de Wit, this is the only one of its kind existing in the original form. The two-tiered gallery made maximum use of limited space; the pulpit swings out from beneath the altar pillar. • Mon–Sat 10am–5pm, Sun 1–5pm ☎ 020 624 66 04 • Oudezijds Voorburgwal 40 🚋 4, 9, 16, 24, 25

Sint Nicolaaskerk (F2) This large 1887 neo-baroque church, recently renovated, dominates the Zeedijk area north of the Red Light District opposite Centraal Station, and is the premier Catholic church in Amsterdam. It is the focal point for the Sinterklaas festival (St Nicholas being the presiding saint), which begins in mid-November and marks the beginning of a long Christmas for lucky

Aspects of Amsterdam to send to your friends or keep as souvenirs.

Dutch children. The church has three choirs, two of which perform choral evensong every Saturday at 5pm from September to June (free admission). Many recitals are given on the 19th-century Sauer organ, highlighted in the summer months during the International Organ Concert Series. • Mon and Sat noon–3pm, Tues–Fri 11am–4pm. Sunday Eucharist at 10.30am, Gregorian Vespers 5pm (not in summer) ☎ 020 624 87 49 • Prins Hendrikkade 73 Ⓜ Centraal Station 🚋 1, 2, 4, 5, 9, 13, 16, 17, 24, 25

Schreierstoren (F2) An unaltered part of the 15th-century fortifications, the "Weeping Tower" is said to be where the women waved off Amsterdam's sailors heading for the four corners of the earth. A plaque placed by the Greenwich Village Historical Society of New York records that it was from here that Henry Hudson set sail on April 4, 1609 to found the city that would become New York. • Prins Hendrikkade ☎ 020 428 82 91 Ⓜ Centraal Station 🚋 1, 2, 4, 5, 9, 13, 16, 17, 24, 25

WALKING TOUR: CENTRAL AMSTERDAM

The big square called **Dam** is dominated by the Royal Palace and the Nieuwe Kerk. Walk south along pedestrianized **Kalverstraat**, named after the cattle *(kalver)* market held here in the 17th century. Side roads from the right-hand side of this busy shopping street lead to the beautiful medieval **Begijnhof** convent, containing the Netherlands' oldest wooden house. Continue along Kalverstraat to Muntplein. The medieval **Munttoren**, whose base was part of the old city walls when the Singel was still a defensive moat, was constructed between 1480–87 and once housed the mint. A Hendrick de Keyser spire was added in 1620. Cross the bridge over Rokin and go left up Oude Turfmarkt, passing the **Allard Pierson Museum**, one of Europe's finest archaeological museums. Turn right onto **Grimburgwal**. At the end of this narrow old street, which is home to some of Amsterdam's ritziest jewellery shops, is the entrance to **Oudemanhuispoort**, a tiny covered arcade that has a 19th-century book market and allows a view of the University of Amsterdam's attractive main courtyard. At the far end of the arcade, emerge onto Kloveniersburgwal and head left. Pausing for a quick look inside the splendid Golden Age entrance to the **Oost-Indisch Huis** on Oude Hoogstraat, go across the canal, past the neoclassical **Trippenhuis** built by Justus Vingboons in 1660, and along Nieuwe Hoogstraat. A small passage on the right leads to Hendrick de Keyser's soaring **Zuiderkerk** of 1614. Opposite the church, admire the elegant white façade of 17th-century **Pintohuis** before walking left up St Antoniesbreestraat to Nieuwmarkt and the multi-turreted Gothic **Waag**, or weigh-house, which in its day has also served as the surgeons' guild and a place of public executions. You are now at the top end of Kloveniersburgwal. At No. 26 is the absurdly narrow **Kleine Trippenhuis**; note too the eyecatching wall tablet above the door of No. 34, **De Linnenkist**. Such tablets were used as a way of identifying addresses before the advent of house numbers in the late 18th century. From the north side of the Waag, head up **Zeedijk**, once the haunt of sailors in search of wine, women and song. At No. 1 is the historic bar **In 't Aepjen**. The name means "At the Monkey": it's said that sailors who couldn't settle their bills would leave their pet monkeys as payment. From here it's a 50-m walk to the trams and trains of Centraal Station.

CENTRAL AMSTERDAM 31

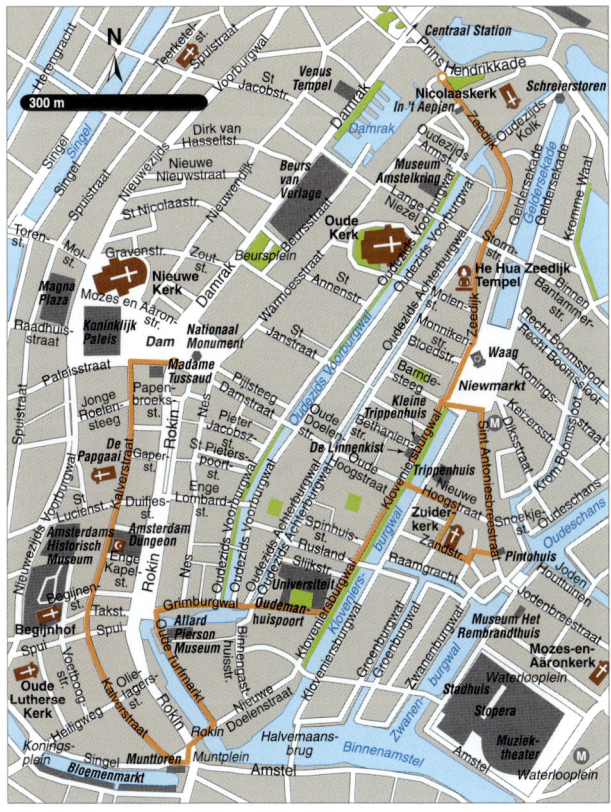

CENTRAL AMSTERDAM
The oldest part of the city

Start: Dam **Finish:** Centraal Station

JORDAAN AND WESTERN GRACHTENGORDEL

The Jordaan district lies on the other side of the Western Grachtengordel, the western part of the main Canal Belt comprised of Singel, Herengracht, Keizersgracht and Prinsengracht, which here are lined with some of Amsterdam's most impressive 17th- and 18th-century merchants' houses. The Jordaan is a very different kettle of herring. It was constructed in the early 17th century to provide housing outside the municipal boundary for workers and foreign refugees, especially Jews and French Huguenots. Indeed, the name Jordaan probably derives from the French word *jardin*: you will notice that several of the streets are named after flowers. Today, with its famous brown cafés, narrow streets and picturesque canals, it has become a magnet for Amsterdam's young professionals, as well as its artists and students.

THE DISTRICT AT A GLANCE

SIGHTS

Architecture
Canal Houses ★ 32
Noorderkerk............34
Westerkerk..............34

Museums
Amsterdam Tulip Museum 34
Anne Frank Huis ★ ...34
Woonbootmuseum..35
Bijbels Museum.......35

WALKING TOUR 36

WINING AND DINING 85

Canal Houses (D 1–2, E1) It's a short walk from Centraal Station to the top of **Singel**, the first and oldest of the main four canals. At No. 7 is one of the city's curiosities, an improbably narrow house. You might wish to compare it to other slimline models further down the canal at No. 144 (under 2 m wide) and No. 166 and ponder what it is like to live in a doll's house. Fans of Rembrandt's *The Night Watch* will want to check out the fine double-gabled house at No. 140–142—it was the home of Captain Frans Banning Cocq, the main figure in the painting.

JORDAAN AND WESTERN GRACHTENGORDEL 33

Soaking up every ray of the sun, a precious commodity in Amsterdam's changeable climate.

The next canal out from Singel is **Herengracht**. At Nos. 170–172 you'll see the magnificent Dutch Renaissance Bartolotti Mansion, with its stunning double-stepped gables. Built in 1617 to a design of Amsterdam's Golden Age Master builder Hendrick de Keyser, note how the house curves beautifully with the canal at this point.

On **Keizersgracht**, the third of the big canals, the Rode Hoed (Red Hat) at No. 102 is a cultural centre located in a beautiful historic building. The Great Hall is the largest and oldest remaining hidden church in the Netherlands. It organizes debates on a wide range of themes as well as lectures and cultural programmes. Almost opposite this is the Huis met de Hoofden (the House of the Six Heads) at No. 123. Local tradition has it that the six carved heads are said to represent burglars who stumbled across a housemaid with a penchant for decapitation (they're actually of the classical muses).

The next canal, **Prinsengracht**, named after the Prince of Orange, borders the Jordaan district. It is the longest of the four main canals.

Noorderkerk (D1) On the Jordaan side of the Prinsengracht, Hendrick de Keyser's unpretentious North Church of 1623 was designed in the shape of a Greek cross and is the only major public building in Jordaan. The square in front of the church plays host to a lively farmers' market on Saturday mornings.
• Su 1.30–5.30pm, Mon 10.30am–1.30pm (piano music), Sat 11am–1pm (organ music) ☎ 020 626 64 36 • Noordermarkt 48 🚋 18, 21 22

Amsterdam Tulip Museum (C2) This small museum is devoted to the country's most famous flower. A film traces the history of the tulip; you can buy bulbs for all kinds of flowers, and souvenirs for all your tulipomaniac acquaintances.
• Daily 10am–6pm • Prinsengracht 112 ☎ 020 421 00 95 🚋 13, 17

Anne Frank Huis (C2) Further down on the other side of Prinsengracht is the house where Anne Frank and her family hid for over two years to avoid Nazi persecution. Entering the secret annex through a revolving bookcase, you pass through the rooms that were both prison and haven until their inhabitants were betrayed and arrested in August 1944. Anne Frank died along with her sister in Bergen-Belsen in March 1945. The Frank family's room still has the wall map on which Anne's father hopefully charted the advance of the Allies from Normandy. The famous diary was written in Anne's small bedroom. It has since been published in more than 55 languages. The rest of the house, run by the Anne Frank Foundation, contains an exhibition on anti-Semitism, and temporary displays monitor the continuing dangers of racism and extremism in modern Europe. The museum gets lots of visitors in summer and you may have to queue. Best to visit in the evening when it's quieter. A statue of Anne Frank by Mari Andriessen stands on the south side of the nearby Westerkerk. • **Mid-March to mid-Sept 9am–9pm, Sat 9am–10pm; mid-Sept to mid-March 9am–7pm, Sat 9am–9pm; Easter weekend, July and August daily 9am–10pm. Last entry 30 minutes before closing. Reduced hours on holidays, see www.annefrank.org** ☎ 020 556 71 05 • Prinsengracht 267 🚋 13, 14, 17

Westerkerk (C2) With the tallest and most dazzling spire in the city, the Westerkerk is unmistakable. The yellow, blue and red crown that tops its 85 m (279 ft) is part of the city's coat of arms, granted to Amsterdam by the Holy Roman Emperor Maximilian I in 1489. Climb to the top for an unparalleled view of the city. The church was built to a plan of Hendrick de Keyser, who died before its completion in 1631. In 1669 the bankrupt Rembrandt was buried here, in an unmarked grave, perhaps with his son Titus, who died the year before and is buried near the memorial to the painter inside the church. The 50-bell carillon (cast in the 17th century by François Hemony) is played every Tuesday from noon to 1pm. Anne Frank, whose house is just around the corner, mentions in her diary being comforted by the sound of the bells. • Mon–Fri 11am–3pm. Friday lunchtime concerts 1pm. Groups can visit outside hours ☎ 020 6247766 • Prinsengracht 281 🚋 13, 14, 17

Woonbootmuseum (C3) Climb aboard the *Hendrika Maria* to see how trim and tidy life can be aboard a typical Amsterdam houseboat. • Mar–Oct Tues–Sun 11am–5pm, rest of year Fri, Sat, Sun, same hours. ☎ 020 427 07 50 • Prinsengracht, opposite No. 296 🚋 7, 10, 17

Bijbels Museum (D4) Possibly the best thing about this museum is its location in two fine canal houses built in the 1660s by the influential Amsterdam architect Philips Vingboons. One room has a ceiling painted by Jacob de Wit; downstairs are kitchens dating back to the 17th century. The exhibition includes a Bible room, with the first printed Dutch Bible from 1477, an Israel in Egypt display, and a model of the temple in Jerusalem. • Mon–Sat 10am–5pm, Sun 11am–5pm ☎ 020 624 24 36 • Herengracht 366 🚋 1, 2, 5

TULIPOMANIA

Holland's love affair with the tulip has lasted since the 16th century, when seeds from Turkey were first cultivated at the Hortus Botanicus in Leiden. By the 1630s, they had become more valuable than precious jewels and works of art, and were traded on the stock exchange, sometimes at the modern equivalent of £3,000 a bulb! Dealers bought up croploads before harvest time, speculating that their value would go up further, while other tulip stocks were sold on twice and three times before a single flower had blossomed. The inevitable crash came in 1636 and ruined several fortunes. It took regulatory action by the High Court of Holland to regain stability.

WALKING TOUR:
JORDAAN AND WESTERN GRACHTENGORDEL

The delightful **Pastoorbrug** at the intersection of Brouwersgracht and Keizersgracht is a great starting point, with a wonderful view from the bridge south to the Westerkerk. Walk along Brouwersgracht towards Prinsengracht. On the corner, the **Papeneiland** dates from 1641 and is one of Amsterdam's most attractive brown cafés. Notice from this spot the row of fine old red-shuttered **warehouses** belonging to the Groene & Grauwe Valk Company on the other side of Brouwersgracht. Walk down Prinsengracht to **Noorderkerk**, built by Hendrik de Keyser in the unusual design of a Greek cross. Just beyond here is **Westerstraat**, leading away from Prinsengracht. It's one of Jordaan's principal streets, lined with shops, cafés and restaurants. A short way along on the right, the intriguing **Pianola Museum** is packed with early 20th-century pianolas. Cross Westerstraat and turn onto **Tweede** (2e) **Tuindwarsstraat**, with its village-like ambience, chichi shops and cafés, and full-length view of the Westerkerk tower. At the far end the street reaches **Bloemgracht**, a lovely canal shaded by elm trees, where you can zigzag your way south to **Rozengracht**. This isn't the most appealing of Jordaan's streets, but **No. 184** is of interest as the house where Rembrandt was forced to move to from the centre of Amsterdam because of his financial difficulties; he died there in 1669. Carry on south from Rozengracht on Tweede Laurierdwarsstraat to the narrow **Elandsgracht** and turn left towards Prinsengracht. The square where the canals meet is **Johnny Jordaanplein**, named after a popular local singer represented by a bronze bust. On Prinsengracht, facing the square, is the **Woonbootmuseum**, a houseboat dating from 1914. This is a good way of seeing inside this classic Amsterdam form of accommodation. Head up Prinsengracht back to the Westerkerk. On the Keizersgracht side of the church is the **Homomonument**, three pink marble triangular sculptures that commemorate persecuted homosexuals by echoing the pink cloth triangles they had to wear under the Nazis. At this point you can board a tram back to the centre or walk up to the corner of Prinsengracht and Egelantiersgracht for a well-earned coffee or glass of beer at **'t Smalle**, a gorgeous brown café in a converted 18th-century *jenever* distillery.

JORDAAN AND WESTERN GRACHTENGORDEL

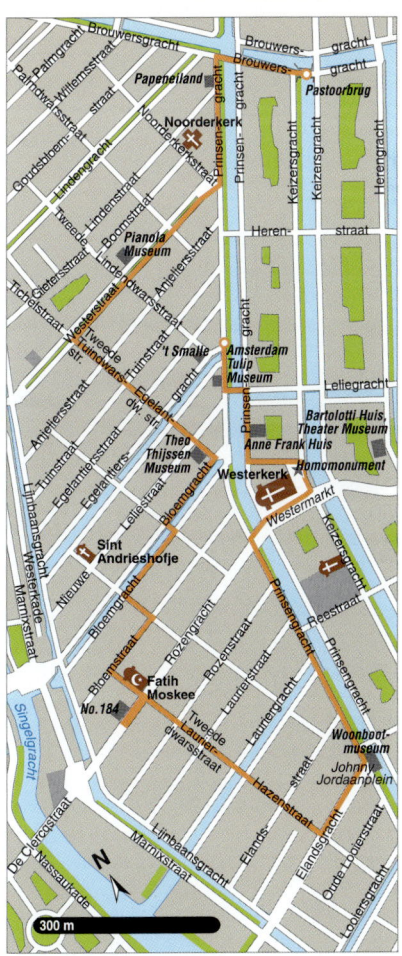

JORDAAN AND WESTERN GRACHTENGORDEL
The Westerkerk from every angle

Start: Pastoorbrug

Finish: Prinsengracht or Egelantiersgracht

CAFÉ CULTURE

The oldest cafés in Amsterdam date from the 1620s, though at the time they would only have served beer and stronger liquors rather than coffee. Coffee clubs, where men gathered to drink coffee and discuss business and the issues of the day, caught on in the 18th century. These were the real forerunners to the café culture we know today.

Brown cafés

Amsterdam's pride and joy is the brown café. With their wood panelling and nicotine-stained walls and ceilings they look as dark and aged as a Rembrandt painting. Some have ancient porcelain beer pumps, others seduce with lead crystal windows painted with scenes of old Amsterdam. There might also be old-fashioned touches like carpet-covered tables and sand on the floors to soak up the beer. The best, like the 1670 **Hoppe** (Spui 18–20), **'t Smalle** (Egelantiersgracht 12) and **De Druif** (Rapenburgerplein 83) give a quintessential experience of traditional Dutch culture and are as cosy and inviting as you could wish a place to be on a cold winter's day.

Coffee shops

Definitely not of the same ilk as coffee houses or ordinary cafés, Amsterdam's coffee shops are more concerned with weed than beans. Found all over the city, but particularly prominent in the tourist streets around the Red Light District and Damrak, these cafés are where marijuana is available to be purchased and smoked—or, as "space cookies", eaten. They are generally identifiable by the Jamaican flag (red, gold, green) in the window, though it's hard not to be aware when you're standing outside one due to the pungent aroma that hangs on the air. New regulations aiming to ban tourists from these establishments have not yet been implemented.

Eetcafés

Exemplifying the Dutch's admirably direct use of language, an *eetcafé* is very much what it says on the label: a café where you eat. In practice, this means that the grub will be taken more seriously in one of these places than in a standard café or brown café. It's guaranteed to be hearty and Dutch—and your waistline is sure to be pushed to the limit.

Grand Cafés

Amsterdam's Grand Cafés gesture towards a world beyond the city; towards the south, in fact, and a notion of Parisian style and grandeur. As such, they tend to be spacious and high-ceilinged, with an emphasis on smart furnishings and good viewing spots, including a wide terrace in summer. The main reason to go to a Grand Café, of course, is to see and be seen by everyone else. Essential venues for this include the Belle Epoque style **L'Opera** on Rembrandtplein, the sumptuous Art Deco **Café Americain** on Leidseplein, and the **Café Luxembourg**, Spui 24.

Theatre café

The cafés attached to Amsterdam's theatres are not only handy for a drink and a bite to eat before or after a performance, but are also attractive, atmospheric places in their own right. The **Felix Meritis Café** has fine views over the Keizersgracht and pulls in many of the performers from around the world who play at the theatre. **Café Vertigo**, part of the Filmmuseum in the Vondelpark, has a subterranean, art-house feel and attracts a suitably trendy cinematic crowd. The **Café Dantzig** is in the Stopera and makes great use of the waterside setting. The Muziekgebouw aan 't IJ in the Eastern Docklands has the dazzling, ultra-modern **Star Ferry Café**.

Proeflokalen

The *proeflokaal* was originally a tasting bar where potential customers would sample liquor such as *jenever*—Dutch gin—before purchasing in greater quantity to take away. Because of this there was just a narrow bar with no seating. You will still have to stand at the **Wijnand Fockinck** (Pijlsteeg 31) and **De Drie Fleschjes** (Gravenstraat 16), two 17th-century *proeflokalen*, where your glass of *jenever* is drawn from a large cask mounted on the wall.

/ **CITYSIGHTS**

SOUTHERN GRACHTENGORDEL AND THE AMSTEL

The southern part of the Grachtengordel has a number of fascinating museums located in beautiful old canal houses covering everything from Golden Age furnishings to cats and handbags. But the orderly grandeur of the area is offset by the rumbustious neon-lit shenanigans of Rembrandtplein and, just across the River Amstel, the hustle and bustle of the modernist Stopera, set among Amsterdam's biggest and best-known flea market. Before the war, this was the centre of the Jewish quarter. Much has changed since then. The past is not forgotten, though; the Portuguese Synagogue and the Jewish Historical Museum can be visited, along with Rembrandt's fine 17th-century house on Jodenbreestraat.

THE DISTRICT AT A GLANCE

SIGHTS

Architecture
Magere Brug ★ 43
Stopera 43
Portugees Synagoge 44
Mozes en Aäronkerk 44
Montelbaanstoren ...45

Atmosphere
Rembrandtplein 41

Landmark
Munttoren 40
Dockworker Statue ..44

Museums
Kattenkabinet 42
FOAM Fotographie-museum 42
Museum van Loon ★ 42

Tassenmuseum Hendrijke 42
Museum Willet-Holthuysen ★ 42
Joods Historisch Museum 44
Rembrandthuis ★ 45

WALKING TOUR 46

WINING AND DINING 86

Munttoren (E4) Used as a mint in 1672, when war with England and France cut off supplies of money to Amsterdam, the name stuck. Overlooking the famous flower market on the Singel, this is another part of the ancient city wall prettified with one of de Keyser's vaguely oriental spires. The tuneful carillon plays every half hour. Because of its central location, the Munt tends to be one

You can take home bulbs, fresh tulips or wooden ones to last a lifetime.

of those places by which people give directions, so it is worth remembering its exact position in relation to the rest of the city in case you need to ask your way.
• Muntplein 🚋 4, 9, 14, 16, 24, 25

Rembrandtplein (E4) A short walk south from Munttoren along the lively Reguliersbreestraat brings you to the former butter market renamed in honour of the great artist in 1876. In the centre, on a patch of grass, there's a statue of Rembrandt looking slightly lost amid all the noise and bustle. Every tourist wants to have a photo taken with him. Neon-lit, lined with cafés and restaurants, and constantly traversed by trams and taxis, the square was given a costly facelift in 2009. There are some good Grand Cafés here, such as L'Opera and the Ritz, as well as the superb Art Deco Café Schiller. The outside terraces are packed in summer. It might be worth considering a film at the **Theater Tuschinski** on Reguliersbreestraat 26, built in 1921 and with an unbelievably over-the-top Art Deco interior. 🚋 4, 9, 14

Kattenkabinet (D4) On Herengracht, a few minutes south of Rembrandtplein and in view of the Golden Bend, the cat cabinet, created in memory of the founder's remarkable cat John Pierpont Morgan, looks at the role of felines in art and culture throughout the centuries. Prints and paintings by Steinlen, Leonor Fini, Foujita, Picasso and many more, and a host of cat-related objets d'art. • Mon–Fri 10am–4pm, Sat–Sun noon–5pm ☎ 020 626 90 40 • Herengracht 497 🚋 1, 2, 5, 16, 24, 25

FOAM Fotografiemuseum Amsterdam (E5) South of the Kattenkabinet on Keizersgracht, this museum and centre for photography and the new media will interest professional and amateur photographers alike. The museum organizes temporary exhibitions, and serves as a platform for discussions and study. • Daily 10am–6pm, Thurs, Fri till 9pm ☎ 020 551 65 00 • Keizersgracht 609 🚋 16, 24

Museum van Loon (E5) Further east along the canal, the first tenant of this elegant double-size canalside house, built in 1672, was a pupil of Rembrandt, Ferdinand Bol. In 1884 the Van Loons, a merchant family, moved in and stayed until 1945. Much of the furniture, silver, crystal, porcelain, photographs and family portraits on view date from the late 19th century. The carefully tended gardens are also open for visits—note the coach house modelled on a Greek temple. • Wed–Mon 11am–5pm. For visits outside these hours, book on ☎ 020 624 53 55 • Keizersgracht 672 🚋 4, 9, 16, 24, 25

Tassenmuseum Hendrikje (E4) Back up on Herengracht, beyond Rembrandtplein, this bright and quirky museum is devoted to the history of handbags and purses over the past five centuries to the present day, with exhibits ranging from ancient pouches and alms bags to 20th-century Art Deco masterpieces. There are regular temporary special exhibitions and a gallery trail (in Dutch only) to keep the kids amused. • Daily 10am–5pm • Herengracht 573 ☎ 020 524 6452 🚋 4, 9, 24, 25

Museum Willet-Holthuysen (E4) A block away, is this fine Golden Age patrician house, redecorated by Abraham Willet in the neo-Louis XVI style that was popular in the 1860s. There is a delightful 18th-century garden seen to best

The Magere Brug seems transplanted from another era.

effect from the octagonal room on the top floor. • Mon–Fri 10am–5pm, Sat–Sun 11am–5pm ☎ 020 523 18 22 • Herengracht 605 🚋 4, 9, 14, 24, 25

Magere Brug (F5) One of Amsterdam's iconic sights is the "Skinny Bridge", which has linked the two sides of the Amstel river since 1671, though as it's made of wood it has seen several different versions since then. See it at night when it is illuminated by hundreds of lights. • Amstel Ⓜ Waterlooplein 🚋 9, 14

Stopera (E–F4) Across the Amstel River, the waterfront and Waterlooplein area are dominated by the controversial 1980s Stopera, the combined Muziektheater-Stadhuis building, which was reviled by Amsterdammers and led to a riot in 1982. It is for the viewer to decide whether or not its marble and brick curve is stylishly matched to the bend in the Amstel over which it presides, or

jarringly inappropriate to the city at large. But it demonstrates yet again that the Amsterdam authorities do not shy away from facing the new. The complex has a good café with riverside terrace from which to ponder these and other issues, such as whether or not to buy that second-hand leather jacket at the adjacent Waterlooplein Flea Market before someone else snatches it up.
• Waterlooplein 22 Ⓜ Waterlooplein or 🚋 9, 14

Joods Historisch Museum (F4) A quick walk south of Stopera, the museum is an excellent conversion of four 17th- and 18th-century synagogues into a museum which traces 400 years of Jewish life in the Netherlands. Particularly interesting is a series of paintings from Charlotte Salomon's autobiographical *Life? or Theatre?* The artist died in Auschwitz at the age of 26. • Daily 11am– 5pm ☎ 020 531 03 10 • Nieuwe Amstelstraat 1 Ⓜ Waterlooplein 🚋 9, 14

Dockworker Statue (F4) On the triangular "square" next to the museum, Mari Andriessen's sculpture (*De Dokwerker* in Dutch) of a thick-set working man honours the dockworkers' 24-hour strike in February 1941, a famous show of solidarity in response to the first mass deportation of Jews by the German occupiers. • Jonas Daniël Meijerplein Ⓜ Waterlooplein 🚋 9, 14

Portugees Synagoge (F4) Escaping from the Spanish Inquisition via Portugal, thousands of Sephardic Jews settled in tolerant Amsterdam, and their expertise and hard work contributed greatly to their adopted home's rise to power in the 17th century. The classical-style Portuguese Synagogue (Esnoga), across the road from the Joods Historisch Museum, was designed by Elias Bouman and completed in 1675, at which time it was the largest in the world. Its spacious interior is particularly impressive, with splendid brass chandeliers holding over a thousand candles, lit for special events. The entrance is through a shop. • April–Oct Sun–Fri 10am–4pm, Nov–March Sun–Thurs 10am–4pm, Fri 10am–2pm ☎ 020 624 53 51 • Mr Visserplein 3 Ⓜ Waterlooplein 🚋 9, 14

Mozes en Aäronkerk (F4) The twin-towered neoclassical façade of this imposing 1840 building looms over Waterlooplein. Nowadays it's as much a cultural centre as a church. ☎ 020 622 13 05 • Waterlooplein 207 Ⓜ Waterlooplein 🚋 9, 14

SOUTHERN GRACHTENGORDEL AND THE AMSTEL

A relaxed air of freedom and tolerance floats around the city.

Rembrandthuis (F3) Jodenbreestraat runs behind the church. Rembrandt lived in this attractive early 17th-century house at No. 4 for nearly twenty years, until a decline in his fortunes meant he had to move to the less select Jordaan area. Apart from offering the chance to get a real sense of how the artist lived and worked, the house displays almost his entire output of 290 etchings. Some of the finest are in the anteroom next to the entrance hall, with three self-portraits including one with his wife, Saskia. • **Daily 10am–5pm** • Jodenbreestraat 4–6 ☎ 020 520 04 00 Ⓜ Nieuwmarkt, Waterlooplein 🚋 9, 14

Montelbaanstoren (F3) The Oude Schans canal is opposite the Rembrandthuis, and Hendrick de Keyser's wedding-cake spire on the Montelbaanstoren at the far end of it dominates the vista. We're lucky it's still there. The 43-m (143-ft) clocktower added to a remnant of the medieval defensive wall nearly caused the whole thing to collapse into the canal. Happily, the 17th-century city authorities paid for it to be shored up. • Oude Schans 2 Ⓜ Nieuwmarkt

WALKING TOUR: SOUTHERN GRACHTENGORDEL AND THE AMSTEL

Set off from Amsterdam's **Bloemenmarkt**, the floating flower market. With the Munttoren behind you, turn left onto Leidsestraat and left again onto Herengracht. The prized **Golden Bend** section begins soon after, with No. 475, a sumptuous neoclassical house of 1672, generally acclaimed as the finest of all the mansions. Further along, take a peek at the **Kattenkabinet** devoted to all things feline at Herengracht 497. Cross Herengracht at the next bridge and carry on to Keizersgracht. On the right-hand side, the **Museum Van Loon**, at No. 672, is a lovely Golden Age house once inhabited by Rembrandt's pupil, Ferdinand Bol. Continue to the intersection with **Reguliersgracht**: the place where the two canals meet has a view of 15 different canal bridges. Before leaving Reguliersgracht, be sure to look at the house at **No. 57**, which has an unusual carved wooden façade and gable dating from 1879. Head back up towards Herengracht. Ahead of you are the bright lights of Rembrandtplein where you can pose and people-watch at **L'Opera**, a Belle Epoque Grand Café. Otherwise, turn right onto Herengracht, passing the **Tassenmuseum Hendrijke** and, in the next block, the **Museum Willet-Holthuysen**, a splendid Louis XVI-style mansion with an 18th-century garden. A short distance from here, the canal runs into the Amstel. Cross the river via the ornate **Blauwbrug**, dating from 1884 and modelled on Paris's Pont Alexander III. Look down the Amstel from here for a view of the city's best-known bridge, the **Magere Brug**, or "Skinny Bridge", a wooden raised bridge that's lit up at night by hundreds of tiny bulbs. On the other side of the river, trace your way around the **Stopera**, the combined town hall and opera house whose design caused huge protests in the 1980s. The music theatre here often has free lunchtime concerts on Tuesdays, but there's always free entertainment to be had just by wandering around the adjacent **Waterlooplein Flea Market**. Behind the Stopera, on Jodenbreestraat, is the **Rembrandtshuis** museum. Metros and trams return you to the centre from Waterlooplein, though you might want to linger a while at **De Sluyswacht**, a lovely old café located in a 17th-century lock-keeper's house and with a marvellous view down the **Oudeschans** to the medieval Montelbaanstoren.

SOUTHERN GRACHTENGORDEL AND THE AMSTEL 47

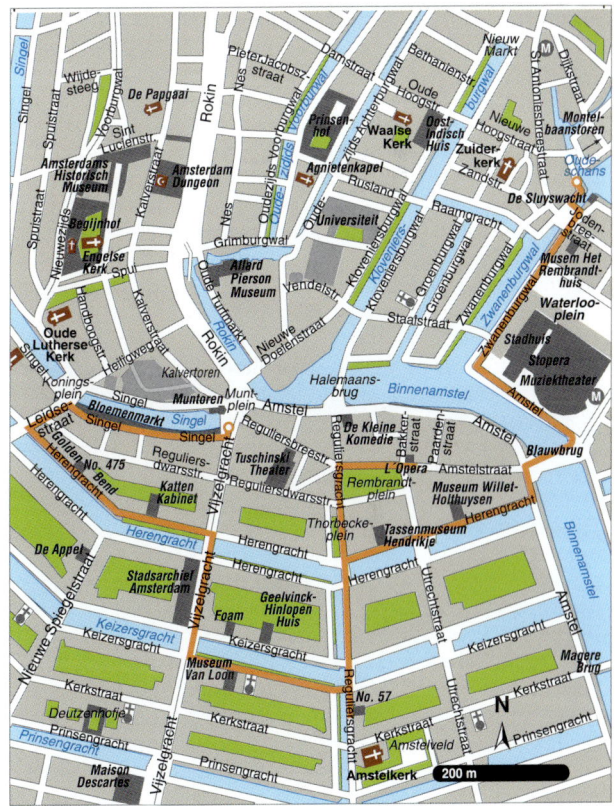

SOUTHERN GRACHTENGORDEL AND THE AMSTEL
A glimpse of the Golden Age

Start: Flower market **Finish:** Jodenbreestraat

IN THE MARKETPLACE

Amsterdammers love markets, and the city has enough of them to sate the appetite of the keenest rummager. In many ways they mirror the wider shopping culture of the city. There are general markets, selling everything from clothes and food to second-hand bicycles and souvenir clogs; and then more specialized ones, which are great places to buy items specific to Amsterdam: flowers, antiques, old books, maps and stamps. As ever, the key market motto should be *caveat emptor*—but if you can sort the wheat from the chaff, you might come away with a bargain. Whatever the outcome, visiting a market in Amsterdam is a lively and enjoyable experience, a good way to see the locals at full bartering throttle.

Common markets

Located along almost the entire length of **Albert Cuypstraat** in De Pijp, the Albert Cuypmarkt is Amsterdam's largest general market, where you'll find a fine selection of herbs, cheese, and exotic spices alongside household goods and second-hand and new clothes at very competitive prices. It's open daily except Sunday and attracts a local crowd—which in cosmopolitan De Pijp means people from just about every continent on earth.

Noordermarkt, a more low-key general market around the Noorderkerk in Jordaan, is held on Monday mornings. It's known for its inexpensive jewellery, clothing, hats, fabrics, and, if you're lucky, the occasional bargain-priced antique. On Saturdays the same location hosts a bird market and, afterwards, a farmer's market selling organic produce.

Nearby **Westermarkt**, on Westerstraat has vast quantities of cheap clothing, plastic kitchenware and other household goods for those keen on looking after the pennies. It's also good place to soak up some true Jordaan ambience. Stalls are in place every Monday 9am–1pm.

Occupying the area around the Stopera, the **Waterlooplein Flea Market** brings in a mix of the dreadlocked and the dropped out, the cool and the curious, and the fashionable and the foreign. It's strong on musical instruments and recordings, books, biker jackets and Indonesian batik, New Age folderol and eccentric bric-a-brac. Prices can be a little steep, but that's just the cost of admission for an entertaining market with a superb location by the Amstel. It's open every day except Sunday 9am–5pm.

Upmarket markets

The **Oudemanhuis Book Market** is one of Amsterdam's most intriguing specialist markets. It's in a tiny alley between Oudezijds Achterburgwal and Kloveniersburgwal and has been the place to go for rare books, prints and sheet music since the 19th century. Book collectors can get their kicks there Mon–Fri 10am–4pm.

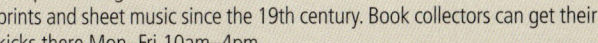

The Netherlands is, of course, famous for its flowers, and in particular its tulips, which have been grown here since the 17th century. Amsterdam's famous floating **Bloemenmarkt**, on permanently moored barges on the Singel between Muntplein and Koningsplein, is not only a colourful sight in the heart of the city, but also amazingly good value, given its magnetic appeal for tourists. You will find cut flowers, bulbs, seeds, pots and bonsaï. Mon–Sat 9.30am–5pm.

Also on a green theme, the **Plantenmarkt**, on Amstelveld, specializes in plants, along with pots and vases to put them in. It opens on Mondays between Easter and Christmas. Occupying a traffic island in front of the Nova Hotel on Nieuwezijds Voorburgwal, the **Stamp and Coin Market** will appeal to stamp, postcard, medal or coin collectors. It's open on Wed and Sat 10am–4pm.

Amsterdam is a haven for lovers of antiques, with a long tradition of top-class craftsmanship in silver, gold and diamonds. At the indoor **Looier antiques market** on Elandsgracht there are stalls selling antique clocks, jewellery, furniture and artworks. Sat–Thurs 11am–5pm.

Queen's Day Market

The biggest market of all is held for just one day each year on the Koninginnedag—the Queen's birthday on April 30th. On this day, every Amsterdammer is allowed to set up stall outside his or her house, resulting in the whole city being transformed into one gigantic flea market. If possible, don't miss it—especially as it goes hand-in-hand with lots of music making, boozing and general merriment.

PLANTAGEBUURT AND DOCKLANDS

Leafy, residential Plantage has been an affluent district ever since it was developed in the 19th century on the back of vast fortunes made in the newly discovered diamond mines of South Africa. Many of those who moved here were Jewish, as the diamond profession was one of the few open to them. The community was virtually wiped out by the German occupiers in World War II. North of the Plantage is the source of an earlier tide of wealth that flowed into Amsterdam, the vast docks and warehouses of the Dutch East India Company. The Docklands are now undergoing major redevelopment and contain some of the city's most radical new architectural wonders.

THE DISTRICT AT A GLANCE

SIGHTS

Architecture
ARCAM 52
IJburg 53

Greenery
Hortus Botanicus ★ .. 50

Museums
Hermitage
Amsterdam 51

Hollandsche
Schouwburg 52
Verzetsmuseum 52
Nationaal
Vakbondsmuseum ... 52
Het Scheepvaart-
museum 52

NEMO ★ 53

Zoo
Artis 51

WALKING TOUR 54

WINING AND DINING 88

Hortus Botanicus (F4) Developed from 1682 in response to the need for new medicinal plants, and enriched by the Dutch East India Company's trade throughout the world, the Botanical Gardens became a vast research laboratory for pioneering scientists such as Linnaeus, Commelin and de Vries. Look out for the Cycad palm in the palm house, one of the original imports from 300 years ago, and probably the oldest potted plant in the world. • Mon–Fri 9am–5pm; Sat, Sun 10am–5pm; July and Aug to 7pm; Dec and Jan to 4pm ☎ 020 625 90 21 • Plantage Middenlaan 2A 🚊 6, 9, 14

People can sail right up to their front door in the Eastern Docklands.

Artis (G–H4) Opened in 1838, the zoo has over 750 species of animals. Particularly impressive are the aquarium and reptile house, the African savannah and the wolves' lair. There are also Geological and Zoological museums (entry via the Aquarium building) and a Planetarium. • Nov–March daily 9am–5pm, April–Oct 9am–6pm. Every Sat in June, July and Aug till dusk. Extra activities on summer evenings called ZOO meravonden ☎ 0900 278 47 96 • Plantage Kerklaan 38–40 🚋 9, 10, 14 or Artis Expres boat from Centraal Station

Hermitage Amsterdam (F4) A satellite of the St Petersburg Hermitage, in the monumental 17th-century Amstelhof building, a former nursing home. The façade, which was the longest in the city in 1683, is unchanged, but the interior has been stripped and remodelled to display items from the Russian collections, in temporary exhibitions. There is an educational studio in the attic, and a Children's Hermitage next door. • Daily 10am–5pm, Wed to 8pm ☎ 020 530 74 88 • Nieuwe Herengracht 14 🚋 9 Ⓜ Waterlooplein

Hollandsche Schouwburg (G4) The Schouwburg theatre, on the edge of the old Jewish quarter, opened in 1892 and came to specialize in Dutch drama. In 1941, however, the Germans made it an exclusively Jewish venue, prior to its final use as an assembly point for Jews from all over Holland before their deportation to the concentration camps. Only the façade survives intact. Inside is a small, poignant exhibition on the theatre and the local Jewish community leading up to their destruction. • Daily 11am–4pm ☎ 020 531 03 40 • Plantage Middenlaan 24 🚋 9, 14

Verzetsmuseum (G4) The Resistance Museum is dedicated to the various strategies employed for counteracting the German occupation 1940–45 through objects, photos, documents, films and audio fragments, and also includes a presentation about the Dutch East Indies • **Tues–Fri 10am–5pm, Sat–Mon 11am–5pm** ☎ 020 620 25 35 • Plantage Kerklaan 61 🚋 7, 9, 14

Nationaal Vakbondsmuseum (G4) Designed by Berlage as the headquarters of the Diamond Workers' Union, the beautiful building with brick arches, murals, ceramics and leaded windows is another of his Modernist wonders, now used for the National Trade Unions Museum. The exhibition is mostly in Dutch. • **Tues–Fri 11am–5pm, Sun 1–5pm** ☎ 020 624 11 66 • Henri Polaklaan 9 🚋 7, 9, 14

ARCAM (G3) Anyone interested in Amsterdam's architecture should visit the modern Architectural Centre. It holds temporary exhibitions and hosts a series of lectures, while the staff can provide information about the future development of the city. • **Tues–Sat 1–5pm** ☎ 020 620 48 78 • Prins Hendrikkade 600 🚋 7, 9, 14

Het Scheepvaartmuseum (G3) Set in a vast naval warehouse of 1656 next to Oosterdok, this museum is informative, well-organized, with a fine collection of paintings of sea battles, model ships, navigational instruments, maps, and gives a thorough picture of the Dutch East India Company's activities in 12 new exhibitions. Highlights include Ferdinand Bol's famous portrait of the sturdy Admiral Michael de Ruyter and a full-size replica of the *Amsterdam*, a fully rigged 18th-century East Indiaman. • **Daily 9am–5pm** ☎ 020 523 22 22
• Kattenburgerplein 1 • 🚌 22, 42, 43

The Science Center, NEMO, was designed by Renzo Piano.

NEMO (G2) The buzzwords here are interactive and hands-on. The ship-shaped technology museum, located on the Oosterdok, promises an upbeat, up-to-the-minute encounter with science and technical gadgetry, with a special interest in energy, communications and the ever-amazing world of the human race. • **Tues–Sun 10am–5pm, school holidays daily 10am–5pm** ☎ 020 531 32 33 • Oosterdok 2 • 🅑 22, 42, 43

IJburg (off map by H1) A whole new residential area is undergoing construction on seven artificial islands of dredged sands in the IJmeer, a lake on the east side of Amsterdam. When completed, there will be 18,000 dwellings for 45,000 inhabitants, together with schools, shops, leisure centres, restaurants, a beach—and a cemetery. The urban design is based on a grid of rectangular blocks, straight streets, green strips and waterways. The first residents moved into their houses in 2002. Several bridges link the islands to the mainland, one of which, the Nesciobrug, is reserved for pedestrians and cyclists. 🚋 26

WALKING TOUR: PLANTAGEBUURT AND DOCKLANDS

In the Plantage district, **Wertheimpark** was at the heart of the pre-war Jewish Quarter. It contains a glass monument to Jewish victims of the Nazi occupation bearing the words *Nooit meer Auschwitz*—"never another Auschwitz". Before leaving the park, it's well worth having a quick look at the **Hortus Botanicus**, which was founded in the 17th century as a means of exploiting tropical plants for medicinal purposes. Walk northwards along Plantage Parklaan and turn right onto Henri Polaklaan, where you will immediately be confronted by the extraordinary façade of H.P. Berlage's **Nationaal Vakbondsmuseum**, built for the Diamond Workers' Union in 1900, complete with modernist crenellations and diamond-shaped pinnacles. At the end of Henri Polaklaan you'll see the domed roof of the Planetarium inside 19th-century **Artis Zoo**. Turn left here onto Kerklaan, which leads to **Entrepotdok**. The dock is lined by a vast row of warehouses that once stored the abundance of exotic goodies traded by the Dutch East India Company. They have now been converted into trendy offices and apartments. Head north through café-lined Kadijksplein to emerge at the large dockland area of the Oosterdok. Opposite, on Kattenburgerstraat, **Het Scheepvaartmuseum**, newly renovated, is located in the former sea arsenal of the United Provinces and dates from 1656. The nautical theme is carried on in the design of **NEMO**, the green, ship-like technological museum that sits above the entrance to the IJ-Tunnel and juts out into the Oosterdok. From the left side of NEMO, walk across a small footbridge to Oosterdokskade and follow the road right to where another footbridge gives access to the **Eastern Islands**. There's a considerable amount of building going on in this area at the moment, and much of it radically modernistic and very definitely cutting edge. Nothing exemplifies this more than the sleek, green lines of the new **Muziekgebouw aan 't IJ** on the western edge of the island overlooking the river. Enter the building to admire the breathtaking central atrium and finish off your walking tour with a drink at the **Star Ferry Café**, with its acres of glass panelling and a waterfront terrace. It's a 10-minute walk to Centraal Station from here, or if you prefer, take a tram from in front of the Muziekgebouw.

PLANTAGEBUURT AND DOCKLANDS
Parkland and docklands close to the river IJ

Start: Wertheimpark
🚋 9, 14 from Centraal Station

Finish: Muziekgebouw aan 't IJ

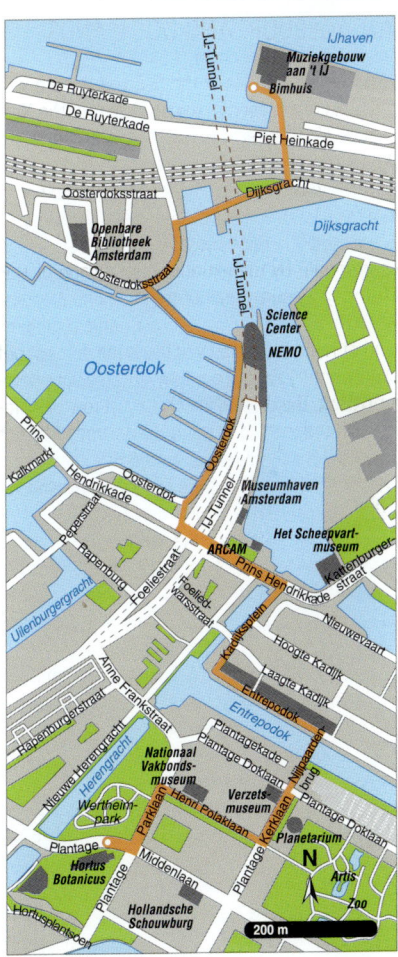

FOR THE CHILDREN

Amsterdam's easygoing attitude towards life extends emphatically to children, who are usually well catered for in restaurants, cafés, museums, concerts and parks. There's always plenty to see and do in the city for kids of all ages.

Wheels and water

Rent a bike and get the kids pedalling around town—they'll love the sense of freedom it gives. If you have smaller children you can always get a bike with a child seat on the back, which is a great, hassle-free way of reaching sights that are further afield. A less strenuous way of seeing the city centre, and one that's always popular with younger children, is a **boat tour** of the canals. But this is Amsterdam, and so there is a cycling alternative even on the water. The **Canal Bike** allows you to pedal along your own route around the canals and, with a good chance of getting severely splashed into the bargain, is unbeatable fun. You can hire one at the Rijksmuseum and Leidseplein jetties.

Outside, inside

The delights of **Vondelpark** include a great playground, lots of open spaces for ball games, and, in summer, a free afternoon programme of music, mime and acrobatics for kids. South of the centre, **Amstelpark** has a children's farm, pony rides, mini golf and can be criss-crossed on a miniature train. The vast **Amsterdamse Bos** offers a petting zoo, boating lakes and some impressively large playgrounds, including the Fun Forest where you can climb through the treetops.

With its big cats and gorillas, reptile house and massive aquarium, **Artis Zoo** will appeal to every member of the family. It also has enough indoor activities to keep kids happy in bad weather, something equally and triumphantly achieved by **Tunfun**, located in an underpass near Visserplein. It has trampolines, a football pitch, café, and is without question the trendiest urban playground in the country.

Cool museums

The hottest ticket in town for kids is **NEMO**, filled with enough hands-on gadgetry and interactive technological wizardry to satisfy every budding Einstein. And they will love clambering over the good **ship** *Amsterdam*, moored outside Het Scheepvaartmuseum. Soccer-mad teenagers might prefer the **Ajax Museum**, located inside the ground of Holland's most successful team, or **Het Oranje Voetbal Museum** on Kalverstraat, devoted to the national side and their pioneering of "Total Football". The well thought-out **Tropenmuseum Junior**, the children's section of the museum, has interesting and informative exhibitions looking at how people live in far-flung corners of the globe. Most children will be aware of the story of Anne Frank, and many will identify with the plight of someone of their own age who endured so much. A visit to the **Anne Frank Huis** is guaranteed to be a moving experience.

Colourful art

The bold, brilliant colours and sheer spontaneity of artists such as Karel Appel and Asger Jorn are guaranteed to strike a chord with any kid who's ever wielded a paintbrush. You'll find their remarkable works displayed at the **CoBrA Museum of Modern Art**, located at the end of the No. 5 tram route in Amstelveen. Van Gogh's palette was marked by an equally vivid use of colour, and children almost always respond to his unique style, where chairs quiver with life and sunflowers virtually burst from the canvas. Even better, kids under 12 get in free to the **Van Gogh Museum**, which contains hundreds of his works.

MUSEUMBUURT AND LEIDSEPLEIN

Occupying an area within the Old South, an affluent residential district developed in the 19th century, the Museumplein was first laid out as the site of the 1883 World Exhibition. P.J.H. Cuypers' palatial Rijksmuseum was built soon afterwards, followed by the Stedelijk in 1895. Both are approaching the end of a long period of renovation. The brick-and-glass of the Van Gogh Museum appeared in 1973. Nearby is the city's favourite place to unwind on a warm day, the Vondelpark. This part of Amsterdam is also a major entertainment area, with the Concertgebouw, at the end of Museumplein, renowned for its superb acoustics and regular performances by top-flight orchestras and soloists, and the clubs, bars and restaurants of Leidseplein across the Singelgracht.

THE DISTRICT AT A GLANCE

SIGHTS

Entertainment
Leidseplein..............63
Max Euwe Centrum..................63

Greenery
Vondelpark..............62

Museums
Rijksmuseum★........58
Van Gogh Museum★..............60
Diamant Museum....61

House of Bols..........61
Stedelijk Museum★.62

WALKING TOUR 64

WINING AND DINING 88

Rijksmuseum (C–D6) If you've already seen Centraal Station, one look at this museum, purpose-built in 1885 for the Netherlands' greatest art collection, tells you that it is the work of the same architect, P.J.H. Cuypers. With entrances on two sides and more than 250 rooms, it is a dauntingly vast building. The restoration works are expected to last until 2013, but you can still see some of its finest masterpieces in the redesigned Philips Wing, while other works are displayed in a new gallery at Schiphol airport.

The museum has fine collections of sculpture and applied art, including Chinese and Japanese porcelain and Delftware, and an excellent display devoted to Dutch history, but what distinguishes the Rijksmuseum is the best collection

The children will have no trouble finding something to amuse them.

of Dutch Masters in the world. Most famous of all is Rembrandt's *The Night Watch*, painted in 1642 when he was 36. Here, among Civil Guard paintings by other Dutch artists, you can see why it is so special—Rembrandt's fascination with the aesthetic implications of light and shade, coupled with a dramatic sense of composition, makes his fellow artists look one-dimensional by comparison. There are many other fine paintings by Rembrandt to be seen. In particular, don't miss his *Self Portrait as the Apostle Paul*, for which he dons a turban; an early portrait of his wife, Saskia; the powerful *Peter's Denial of Christ*; the compositionally masterful *De Staalmeesters*; and one of his late works, *The Jewish Bride* (1666). There are four exquisite paintings by Vermeer, ranging from the photographic detail of *The Little Street* to the remarkable intimacy of *Woman Reading a Letter* and *The Kitchen Maid*. The gallery also has several works by the ever-popular Frans Hals, Jan Steen's pictures of rumbustuous drinking parties, Avercamp's winter scenes, and paintings by Jacob van Ruisdael, Pieter de Hooch, Ferdinand Bol and Nicolaas Maes. All in all, there is no better introduc-

ART OF DARKNESS

The Night Watch is one of the best-known paintings in the world of art, but would it have been so memorable if it were only known by its correct title, *The Company of Captain Frans Banning Cocq and Lieutenant Willem van Ruytenburch?* The catchier nickname came about in the 19th century because the painting had by then acquired a thick coating of dirt, which made the scene look several shades darker than Rembrandt had painted it. Fortunately, the picture was recently cleaned, and now stands at the heart of the Rijksmuseum's collection in its original glory.

tion to classic Dutch painting and culture in general. • Daily 9am–6pm, Fridays late closing 9.30pm ☏ 020 674 70 00 • Jan Luijkenstraat 1 🚋 2, 5, 6, 7, 10

Van Gogh Museum (C6) For fans of Van Gogh this is close to paradise—the world's largest collection of his work, in a glassy modern building designed by Gerrit Rietveld. The adjoining asymmetric wing by Japanese architect Kisho Kurokawa was inaugurated in 1999 and is used for temporary exhibitions. On the first floor of the main building, the larger canvasses are laid out in chronological order, following Van Gogh southwards from the sombre brown of his first masterpiece, *The Potato Eaters*, painted in 1885 while he was still in his native Brabant, through the brighter *Hill of Montmartre* with a *Quarry* done in Paris the following year, until he arrives in the South of France in a dazzling flourish of colour and heightened expression with such works as *Sunflowers*, *The Yellow House*, and *The Bedroom at Arles*. There are also five of the remarkable self-portraits, studies after Millet and Rembrandt, and his extraordinary last paintings, the ominously dark *Wheatfield with Crows*, and near-abstract *Undergrowth*. The second floor is a study area, with access to the museum's web site and a number of art books. There is also a changing display of prints. On the ground and third floors, the museum exhibits works by other 19th-century artists, such as Pierre Bonnard, Gustave Caillebotte, Gustave Courbet, Kees van Dongen, Claude Monet and Paul Gauguin. • Daily 10am–6pm, Fri to 10pm ☏ 020 570 52 00 • Paulus Potterstraat 7 🚋 2, 3, 5, 12, 16

Diamant Museum (C6) A dazzling display devoted to a girl's best friend, illustrating the lifetime of a diamond from the deposits made 3 billion years ago through mining, polishing, setting and design, with a special section devoted to spectacular robberies. • **Permanent and temporary exhibitions. Daily 9am–5pm** ☎ 020 305 53 00 • Paulus Potterstraat 2–8 🚋 2, 5

House of Bols (C6) The Bols family established their first distillery way back in 1575, devoting their attention to liqueurs. They started making *jenever*, sold in those famous stone bottles, 100 years later. Here you will discover the relationship between taste and smell in the Hall of Taste, learn how to mix a good

DIAMONDS ARE TRUMPS

Amsterdam became a centre for diamonds 400 years ago, after the Spanish attacked Antwerp. The diamond traders, knowing what was good for them, beat a hasty retreat north. Later, they were joined by Jewish refugees from the East, for whom diamond cutting was one of the few professions not barred to them by city trade guilds. The work was hard and dirty, but the Jewish Quarter rapidly developed into the heart of Amsterdam's diamond business. Boom time arrived in the 1870s with the opening up of the South African diamond fields. It was said that Dutch diamond workers lit their cigars with 10f notes. The Cullinan Diamond, the largest ever found, and the Koh-i-Noor, part of the British Crown Jewels, were both cut in Amsterdam during this period. The good times couldn't last. A slump in the market in the early 20th century, followed by the German assault on the Jewish population in the 1940s, meant things would never be the same again. But Amsterdam is still a major diamond centre, and you can visit diamond-polishing factories, such as the Amsterdam Diamond Center, Rokin 1–5, ☎ 020 624 57 87; Gassan Diamonds, Nieuwe Uilenburgerstraat 173–175, ☎ 020 622 53 33; Coster Diamonds, Paulus Potterstraat 2–6, ☎ 020 305 55 55.

cocktail and improve your bottle-juggling technique in the World of Bartending, an sample a cocktail before visiting the shop where you can buy a starter kit. The entrance fee includes a cocktail in the Mirror bar. • **Daily (except Tues) noon–6pm, Fri to 10pm** ☎ 020 570 85 75 • Paulus Potterstraat 14 🚋 2, 5

Stedelijk Museum (C6) The famous Stedelijk Museum on Paulus Potterstraat has been rebuilt, creating much more display space, a vast entrance hall and an area nicknamed "the bathtub" for cutting-edge exhibitions. Work is still ongoing, but exhibitions entitled "temporary stedelijk 3" are being staged in various locations around the city. The classic collection includes works by Picasso, Cezanne, Chagall and Matisse, as well as a major group of abstract artists such as Mondriaan and Kandinsky. The museum is especially proud of its important collection of works by the Russian artist Kasimir Malevich. Art since 1945 is well represented with paintings by the Dutch-American Willem de Kooning, Andy Warhol, Georg Baselitz, Roy Lichtenstein, Barnett Newman and many others.
• **For details of the grand re-opening planned for 2012, see www.stedelijk.nl** ☎ 020 573 29 11 • Museumplein 10 🚋 2, 3, 5, 12, 16

Vondelpark (A–B6) Named after the poet Joost van den Vondel, who is commemorated by an imposing statue, this is the city's premier park, a great place to people-watch on a warm summer's day. Civilized and safe, it is full of ponds, pathways, bridges, bandstands and cafés. On Queen's Day on April 30, the park becomes one enormous party, with the emphasis on family entertainment, stalls, barbecues, and music. • **Daily dawn–dusk** 🚋 1, 2, 3, 5, 6, 7, 10, 12

Leidseplein (C5) The site of a medieval city gate on the road to Leiden, this lively square is back across the Singelgracht from Vondelpark, between Singelgracht and Prinsengracht. It's the centre of Amsterdam's nightlife (if you don't count the other variety in the red-light district). Crammed with bars, cafés, nightclubs, and restaurants serving food from all over the globe, it's the place to come to experience Amsterdam at its most exuberant. The square is dominated by the Stadsschouwburg, which puts on concerts and theatre productions (occasionally in English), and the Art-Nouveau American Hotel. Behind the Stadsschouwburg is a relic of the 1960s hippy era, the Melkweg, which today is a successful mix of cinema, music venue, gallery and café.

Max Euwe Centrum (C5) Named after the Netherlands' only world chess champion to date, the Max Euwe Centrum, to the south of Leidseplein, covers the history of chess. Games are organized, or you can test your skills against a computer.
• Tues–Fri and first Saturday of the month noon–4pm ☎ 020 625 70 17 • Max Euweplein 30 a-1 🚋 1, 2, 5, 6, 7, 10

ART WITH BITE

CoBrA refers to a radical group of artists from Copenhagen, Brussels and Amsterdam who came together in 1948 to give the world the shock of the new. Works by Karel Appel, Eugene Brands and Asger Jorn, among others, reflect the group's belief in an art which is spontaneous, primitive, revolutionary. Brushstrokes are bold, colours sensual, paintwork wild and unfettered. The **CoBrA Museum voor Moderne Kunst**, in a modernist gallery at Sandbergplein 1–3, Amstelveen, is at the end of the Tram 5 line, Tues–Sun 11am–5pm.

WALKING TOUR: MUSEUMBUURT

The best way to approach the famous art galleries of the Museum area from central Amsterdam is along **Nieuwe Spiegelstraat** and **Spiegelgracht**, which run south from Herengracht's Golden Bend and are filled with antique shops and art salerooms selling top-end works; from ceramic art and modern abstract paintings to canvases from the 17th-century school of Rembrandt. Spiegelstraat leads directly to the **Rijksmuseum**, whose mighty façade mixes neo-Gothic and neo-Dutch Renaissance elements. The architect was Centraal Station architect PJH Cuypers. During its renovation, the museum displays 200 of the finest paintings from its unparalleled collection of Dutch art, including *The Night Watch* and the four Vermeers. Go to the right of the museum along Jan Luijkenstraat then turn left to reach Paulus Potterstraat. At No. 14, the **House of Bols** has one-hour tours telling you all you need to know about the well-known makers of *advocaat* (eggnog). Further along the same street, the large crowds of tourists will soon let you know you're about to arrive at the modern concrete-and-glass **Van Gogh Museum**. A few steps away, the **Stedelijk** makes up the third part of the Museumbuurt triumvirate. It has a prestigious collection of modern art, though it's being renovated and will open in 2012. At the end of Paulus Potterstraat, go left onto Van Baerlestraat. The **Museumplein**, a large, open expanse with a café, souvenir stalls and a pond, will be on your left, offering a good view of the south side of the Rijksmuseum. The strikingly Gothic elements of the building here were taken as showing too much evidence of Cuypers' grounding in church architecture—the Catholic Church, that is, and Cuypers' Catholicism made him a target for Protestant criticism from the king down. Opposite, the neoclassical **Concertgebouw** is home to the world-class Amsterdam Concertgebouw orchestra. Retrace your steps along Van Baerlestraat to **P.C. Hooftstraat**, Amsterdam's most upmarket fashion street with shops such as Cartier, Louis Vuitton and Ermenegildo Zegna. Continue left along here to **Vondelpark**. Stroll along its lovely paths, check out the rose garden, do a lap of the pond and then stop for a hot chocolate at the circular 1930s **'t Blauwe Theehuis** overlooking the pond, or the **Café Vertigo**, inside the 19th-century pavilion that houses the Filmmuseum.

MUSEUMBUURT AND LEIDSEPLEIN 65

MUSEUMBUURT
Art and advocaat in the museum area

Start: Herengracht

Finish: Vondelpark

DUTCH MASTERS

While the Netherlands has produced few writers or composers of note, it has punched well above its weight in the visual arts. The famous Rijksmuseum, along with smaller gems such as the Civic Guard Gallery and the Amsterdam Museum, offer an encyclopaedic introduction to one of the world's greatest artistic traditions.

Medieval and Renaissance

Many of the finest early Dutch artists were anonymous, commissioned by the Church to paint religious art for altarpieces, such as *The Seven Works of Charity* by the Master of Alkmaar. By the early 16th century, however, there was a steady traffic, both mercantile and cultural, between Holland and Italy, and artists such as Jan van Scorel (1495–1562) and Maerten van Heemskerk (1498–1574) were profoundly influenced by the new humanistic vocabulary of the Italian Renaissance. Though dismissed by Michelangelo as painters of "stuffs and masonry... rivers and bridges," their concern with realism—or "external exactness", as the Italian sniffily put it—can now be seen as one of the essential pillars of Dutch art. A painting like van Scorel's *St Mary Magdalen* in the Rijksmuseum not only demonstrates an impressive grasp of composition and expression learned from Leonardo's *Mona Lisa*, but is also in itself an exquisite work of art.

The Golden Age

One of the effects of the Protestant Reformation in Holland was to put an end to commissions for religious art by the Church. Fortunately, this was more than made up for by the corresponding economic boom of the 17th-century Golden Age, when the newly rich bourgeoisie sought to demonstrate their cultural credentials—and immortalize themselves—by hanging family portraits, landscapes, history and still life paintings on their walls. Art historians have estimated that all but the poorest of households would have had several paintings on display, while shopkeepers decorated their shops with them and guilds and militia groups tickled their vanities with vast group portraits. The laws of supply and demand meant that an army of artists sprang up to satisfy this need. Artists like Frans Hals (1581–1666) worked almost exclusively in portraiture; others, such as Jacob van Ruysdael (1628–82) and Albert Cuyp (1620–91) painted landscapes; Bartholomeus van der Helst (1630–70) is noted for his magnificent *Banquet of the Civic Guard*; Jan Steen (1625–79), Pieter de Hooch (1629–84) and Gerard Terborch (1617–81) were specialists in earthy genre works.

Rembrandt and Vermeer

Towering above these artists are the presiding geniuses of the Golden Age: Rembrandt van Rijn (1606–69) and Jan Vermeer (1632–75). Rembrandt was a master of light and shade and dominated every form he turned his hand to, from the intense psychological realism of his self-portraits to powerful classical and Biblical scenes like *St Peter Denying Christ*, and even the hackneyed Civic Guard genre, transformed into the marvel of the *Night Watch*. Vermeer's tiny output—a mere 35 paintings—is a stunning journey into ultra-realism in terms of detail and technique. Most of his canvases are interiors—the Rijksmuseum's *The Little Street* is a rare exception—and suggest a concern with exploring the moral reality of Dutch life rather than the outside world.

18th Century

Towards the end of the 17th century that outside world came crashing down with a vengeance. Holland was invaded by Louis XIV's troops. The Dutch economy headed into a century of economic downturn, and one of the first casualties of financial belt-tightening was art for private consumption. The final nail in the coffin was the growing obsession with French culture: among the artists who affected the grand, decorative French 18th-century style were Adriaen van der Werff (1659–1722) and Jacob de Wit (1695–1754). To see the best work of this period, check out de Wit's amazing ceiling paintings at the Bijbels Museum.

DE PIJP AND OOSTERPARKBUURT

Head south from the southern Grachtengordel and you are soon pitched into what was once a solidly working class area of workers and their families. More recently it's been enlivened by the arrival of a fairly large immigrant population, as well as attracting a Bohemian mix of artists and students. It's also home to the huge Albert Cuypstraat market and the attractive Sarphatipark. To the east, over the Amstel, is the Oosterpark, and both the park itself and the nearby tropical museum are sure to prove to be highly diverting for young and old alike.

THE DISTRICTS AT A GLANCE

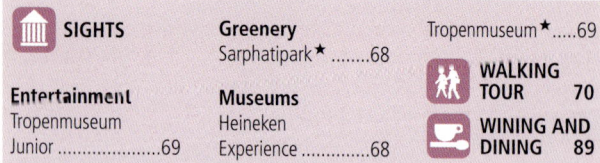

SIGHTS	**Greenery** Sarphatipark ★ 68	Tropenmuseum ★ 69
Entertainment Tropenmuseum Junior 69	**Museums** Heineken Experience 68	**WALKING TOUR** 70 **WINING AND DINING** 89

Heineken Experience (D6) Gerard Heineken moved his brewery *(brouwerij)* here in 1867. By 1988 it had outgrown the site on Stadhouderskade by the Singelgracht, which was turned into a reception centre. The guided tour takes you past huge fermentation tanks, where lively videos and displays tell the history of brewing as well as the story of Heineken itself. Liberal quantities of the company's famous product are on offer at the Heineken bar. The admission fee goes to charity. • **Guided tours: Heineken Experience, Tues–Sun 10am–7pm. Last tour 5.30pm. Children under 18 admitted only under parental guidance** ☎ 020 523 92 22 • Stadhouderskade 78 🚊 16, 24, 25

Sarphatipark (Off map by E6) A charming little park in the heart of the De Pijp area, with a serpentine pond and a brilliant seasonal show of tulips and crocuses. There is also a bronze bust of Dr Sarphati, an enlightened 19th-century entrepreneur. • **Daily dawn–dusk** • Ceintuurbaan 🚊 3, 4, 16, 24, 25

There's a party atmosphere at the Heineken Experience, one of Amsterdam's most popular tours.

Tropenmuseum (H5) From its origins as the Colonial Institute, the Tropical Museum, just north of the Oosterpark, has reinvented itself as a modern establishment dealing with the environmental and social problems of the third world. The ethnographical exhibits from Oceania, the Far East and Indonesia are fascinating. There are also walk-through, life-size street scenes depicting a Bombay slum, modern Jakarta, and rural Africa and India. The museum has been laid out with such exuberance that it is always a hit with children. • **Tues–Sun 10am–5pm** ☎ 020 568 82 00 • Linnaeusstraat 2 🚋 3, 7, 9, 10, 14

Tropenmuseum Junior (H5) Music, singing and dancing classes for children, who bring scenes of the Tropenmuseum Museum to life. After the 75-min programme parents are guided round by their children (6–13 years). • **Wed 1.30 and 3.15pm, Sat, Sun and school holidays 11am, 1.30 and 3.15pm.** Times vary according to the activity. Best to call Reservation ☎ 020 568 82 33 • Linnaeusstraat 2 🚋 3, 7, 9, 10, 14

WALKING TOUR: DE PIJP AND OOSTERPARKBUURT

Start at the **Heineken Experience**, in the brewery like a great brick beer cathedral on the corner of Stadhouderskade and Ferdinand Bolstraat. Production moved outside Amsterdam in 1988 because of lack of space on the site, but the brewery tour and tasting still hits the spot. Continue south along Ferdinand Bolstraat to **Albert Cuypstraat**. Named after the Golden Age landscape painter, it's home to an atmospheric local market whose exotic clientele is matched by the restaurants to be found here, from Surinamese to Cambodian and Kurdish. Turn right at Eerste (1e) van de Helststraat and walk a couple of blocks to the wide Ceintuurbaan for a wander around **Sarphatipark**, which has a long, serpentine lake. Dr Sarphati was responsible for developing this part of the city in ways that were unusually benevolent towards the 19th-century working-class population. De Pijp was originally developed as a working-class quarter of long, narrow streets (hence its name—"the pipe") and poor housing. It's worth making a detour south from Sarphatipark to Pieter Lodewijk Takstraat to see the striking **Dageraad** housing complex. Built just after World War I for poor families of the district, it's a radical architectural solution to the problem, though one typical of Amsterdam, perhaps. Walk north again up to Ceintuurbaan and head right to the Amstel River, where you can cross via the Nieuwe Amstelbrug to the Oosterparkbuurt, or the East Park District. This is named after the dominant feature of the area, the large, rectangular **Oosterpark**. From the bridge, follow the tram line that runs along Ruyschstraat and leads to the park itself, which is a great place to lie on the grass and take the weight off your feet, enjoy the flowers and generally chill out. On the east side of the park, follow Linnaeusstraat north towards the Singelgracht. Just before the canal on the left is the **Tropenmuseum**, which offers imaginative exhibitions about the tropics and has an excellent museum for children as well. Just across the Singelgracht, note the **Muiderpoort**, an 18th-century classical arch built as a gateway. Napoleon entered the city at the head of his troops here in 1811. Strike westwards along the **Mauritskade** running along the south of the Singelgracht to where it meets the Amstel, and unwind over a cold drink at the **Amstelhaven** café, a true haven of peace by the water's edge.

DE PIJP AND OOSTERPARKBUURT

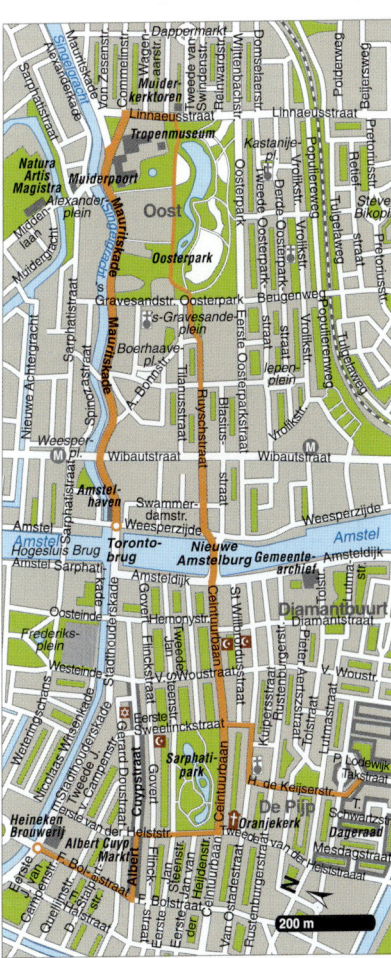

DE PIJP AND OOSTERPARKBUURT
A lively, colourful and cosmopolitan district

Start: Stadhouderskade

Finish: Torontobrug

CURIOSITY SHOPS

One of Amsterdam's greatest specialities is the speciality shop, where items on sale will include everything from the ultra practical to the utterly curious. Needless to say, they make great places to find idiosyncratic and unusual gifts.

To wear...

Unsurprisingly, perhaps, Amsterdam has more than one dedicated clog shop: **'t Klompenhuisje** (Nieuwe Hoogstraat 9a) sports an impressively wide selection; the equally well-stocked **De Klompenboer** (Nieuwezijds Voorburgwal 20) also has a small clog museum.

For the other end of the body, **Donald E. Jongejans** (Noorderkerkstraat 18) is devoted to spectacle frames, many of them virtual antiques and occasionally supplied as props for period movies.

It's all in the wrist action at the **Amsterdam Watch Company** (Reestraat 3), a great little place that sells some of the rarest (and most expensive) brands in the world while also providing an expert watch repair service.

To use...

It's in the area of retail with what one might call "highly focused applications" that Amsterdam's speciality shops really come into their own.

Maranon Hangmatten (Singel 488–490) is Europe's largest hammock store, with South American hammocks in brilliant colours, double hammocks for sharing the experience, hammocks for babies and even ordinary hammocks for those who just want to hang about for a while.

De Witte Tandenwinkel (Runstraat 5) has a far greater range of toothbrushes and flavoured toothpastes than even the most dedicated dental hygienist could dream of.

Feeling amorous? Check out the **Condomerie Het Gulden Vlies** (Warmoesstraat 141), where you'll find condoms in every shape, colour, design, brand and, yes, flavour.

Bugged by mosquitoes? **Bangla Klamboe** (Prinsengracht 232), with a shopful of mosquito nets in a fashionable choice of colours, will be right up your street.

Vlieger (Amstel 34) can sell you Egyptian papyrus or handmade paper with petals and plants woven in. **Vliegertuig** (Gasthuismolensteeg 8), on the other hand, have bright and cleverly designed kites for windy days in the Vondelpark.

A must for smokers is **P.G.C. Hajenius** (Rokin 92–96), which has been selling tobacco for more than 170 years. The shop has a splendid 1920s interior and is famous for its own-brand cigars and Dutch clay pipes. Hypochondriacs and those who like unusual old apothecaries should beat a path to **Jacob Hooij** (Kloveniersburgwal 12). They've been making up potions on this site for two centuries and, with its spice drawers and pots of herbs, it looks as though things haven't changed very much in all that time.

To eat...

Wegewijs Kaas (Rozengracht 32), run by the same family for more than a century, offers more than 100 different Dutch cheeses. Serious chocoholics will be able to get a serious fix at **Hendrikse** (Overtoom 472), suppliers to the Dutch royal family. **Het Oud-Hollandsche Snoepwinkeltje** (Tweerde Egelantiersdwarsstraat 2) sells candies, fruit drops and Dutch liquorice (called *drop*—and it can be sweet or salty), all enticingly displayed in rows of apothecary-style jars.

To drink...

Oscar Wilde claimed that absinthe makes the heart grow fonder. You can put this to the test at two speciality booze shops, **De Cuyp** (Albert Cuypstraat 146) and **Le Cellier** (Spuistraat 116) and see whether the homegrown *jenever* (Dutch gin) does the trick just as well. Beer is king at **De Bierkoning** (Paleisstraat 125), where there are upwards of 800 makes of ale, lager and other brews available. Afterwards you might be in need of a strong cup of coffee. **Geels & Co** (Warmoesstraat 67) and **'t Zonnetje** (Haarlemmerdijk 45) have been serving their customers top quality coffee beans and loose teas from around the world for centuries.

EXCURSIONS

There's more to life than Amsterdam, believe it or not. Beaches, old fishing villages, picturesque Golden Age towns and other major cultural centres are all a short ride away. They can be reached by train or bus from Centraal Station. You can obtain a timetable and further information from the Netherlands Railways (NS) desk inside Centraal Station, or by visiting their website, www.ns.nl. You might also enquire at the VVV office, or contact them on 0900 400 40 40, www.holland.com.

THE REGION AT A GLANCE

SIGHTS

Art and architecture
Haarlem ★ 75
Utrecht 76

Leiden 77
Delft ★ 79
The Hague ★ 80
Rotterdam 80

Seaside
IJsselmeer 74
Zandvoort 76

Tulip Trail
Keukenhof
Bulb Gardens ★ 79

IJsselmeer (map 1) In 1932 the Zuider Zee, the large inland sea to the north of Amsterdam, was cut off by the Afsluitdijk, ending the ancient seafaring tradition of villages such as Marken, Hoorn and Enkhuizen. This only seemed to confirm their reputation as the "dead towns", following the decline from their 17th-century heyday and the overpowering economic success of Amsterdam. Today through tourism and, ironically, their proximity to the capital for commuters, these Golden Age towns and isolated fishing villages live again.

Marken is a picturesque island, joined by causeway to the mainland in 1957. The green and white houses were built on stilts to avoid the floods which were a regular problem before the completion of the Afsluitdijk. Take a look at the Marker Museum, located in four old fish-smoking houses, for a view of the island as it once was. **Edam** is known not only for its cheese but as one of the best preserved of Holland's Golden Age towns. In earlier days it was a wealthy trading and shipbuilding centre, as evidenced by the Grote Kerk and fine canalside houses. **Hoorn** was home to many of Holland's great explorers, such as

Dutch cheeses were made round for easy storing on sailing ships, and the waxy coating was invented to keep moisture in and mould out.

Abel Tasman and Willem Schouten, who first rounded Cape Horn and named it after his birthplace. Don't miss the Westfries Museum located in the Staten-College of 1632, which will fill you in on the history of the West Friesland region. The former whale-fishing port of **Enkhuizen** now boasts one of the best museums in the country, the Zuider Zee Museum. The outdoor part is reached by boat from the main jetty, and consists of over 100 original buildings relocated from around the old Zuider Zee. • **Marken**: 15 km northeast; 30 min by bus 111 • **Edam**: 20 km north; 35 min by bus 114 • **Hoorn**: 33 km northeast; 40 min by train • **Enkhuizen**: 45 km northeast; 55 min by train • Trains from Centraal Station; buses can be boarded outside.

Haarlem (map 1) An extremely pretty town with cobbled streets, several picturesque *hofjes*, and its own proud history. The **Grote Kerk** of St Bavo has a magnificent Gothic interior, with a finely carved choir screen. The Christopher Muller organ, built in the 1730s, 30 m (98 ft) high and with over 5,000 pipes,

SAY CHEESE

Edam, Gouda and Alkmaar all have picturesque summer cheese markets, where the porters dress in traditional white costume and lacquered straw hats and carry huge piles of cheese on large wooden sleds hung from their shoulders. The buyers taste from the flat wheels of Gouda or round balls of yellow Edam (they're only cased in red for export), and when a deal is struck the porters cart their loads into the ancient *kaaswaag* to be weighed.

was played by both Handel and Mozart. Nearby, the **Vleeshal** meat market is one of Holland's great Renaissance buildings. Not long before its construction, the artist Frans Hals settled in Haarlem. The **Frans Hals Museum** is situated in the Oudemannenhuis (an almshouse for old men), and has a fine collection of Civic Guard portraits by Hals, as well as his late paintings of the Oudemannenhuis's governors. The **Teylers Museum**, founded in 1778, is Holland's oldest, and as well as its collection of fossils and crystals there are over 4000 drawings by Michelangelo, Raphael and Rembrandt, among others. • 20 km west; trains take 17 min direct from Centraal Station. VVV Haarlem, Stationsplein 1, ☎ 0900 616 16 00

Zandvoort (map 1) This pleasant seaside resort is popular with Amsterdammers, who don't mind the crowded beaches in summer. To the north, international championship meetings are held on the motor-racing track. • 30 km west; trains take 30 min direct from Centraal Station.

Utrecht (maps pp.1, 2) This compact university city is easy to visit on foot. Or by boat, as the Old Town is laced with shady canals. Most of Utrecht's life centres on the Oudegracht canal or the vast Vredenburg square. Over it all looms the **Dom**, with the tallest and finest church tower in the country. The bells play a tune every quarter-hour, and if you care to climb up the 465 steps, you'll have a breathtaking view over the town. The same religious instinct that inspired the people to build the cathedral convinced them to provide for their poor and elderly—look for the **almshouses** of the Bruntenhof,

Some Dutch people still wear klompen *for working in the garden, though they are mostly made for the tourist trade nowadays.*

Beijerskameren and Mieropskameren. The **Central Museum**, occupying the former Convent of Saint Agnes, harbours a fine collection of painting and decorative arts. Another convent houses the **Catharijneconvent Museum**, filled with ecclesiastical art. Fans of the De Stijl 1920s movement—all right angles as in a Mondrian painting—should take a look at its embodiment in the superimposed rectangular prisms of the **Rietveld Schröder house**. • 39 km (24 miles) southeast; trains take 30 min from Centraal Station. VVV Utrecht, Domplein 9 ☎ 0900 128 87 32 or Lange Viestraat 311 ☎ 030 236 00 00

Leiden (map 1) The Netherlands' oldest university was founded here in the 1570s and became a centre for foreign dissenters. The Pilgrim Fathers lived here before sailing to America. Their leader, John Robinson, is buried in the Pieterskerk. Be sure to visit the **Hortus Botanicus**, planted in 1587, where the first tulips in Holland were cultivated. There are several fine museums, not least the **Rijksmuseum van Oudheden**, with its displays of Egyptian, Greek and Roman artefacts.

The **Lakenhal** has paintings by Lucas van Leyden (his remarkable Last Judgement triptych), Jan Steen and Rembrandt, all of whom were born in the city. • 40 km southwest; trains take 35 min direct from Centraal Station VVV Leiden, Stationsweg 2d ☎ 0900 222 23 33

Keukenhof Bulb Gardens (map1) A trip from Amsterdam to The Hague between late March and late May will take you through an amazing tulip trail. The best place to head for is the Keukenhof, once the kitchen garden of the 15th-century Countess Jacoba van Beieren. Set up in 1949 by Holland's bulb growers as a showpiece for their business, it looks magnificent. Here, over 7 million daffodils, hyacinths and, of course, tulips seduce the senses. In nearby Lisse, the **Museum voor de Bloembollenstreek** tells the tulip's colourful history in the Netherlands. • 27 km southwest; Connexxion Bus Company runs a Schiphol–Keukenhof shuttle every 15 minutes, 🅱 58. From the centre of Amsterdam 🅱 370 or 197 takes you to Schiphol (info ☎ 0900 92 92). It is an all-in Bus and Keukenhof ticket. Alternatively, ask at VVV Amsterdam for details of excursions.

Delft (maps 1, 3) An irresistibly attractive town, with tree-lined canals, fine Golden Age houses, and a picturesque marketplace. Delft is most famous for its blue-and-white pottery. Be sure to check out one of the working factories such as **De Porceleyne Fles**, Rotterdamseweg 196, founded in 1653. Delft was the birthplace of the painter Jan Vermeer, who is buried in the 13th–14th-century Gothic **Oude Kerk**. Its leaning tower is hard to miss. If you also

◀ *Don't miss a visit to the Keukenhof tulip gardens.*

visit The Hague you can compare his marvellous *View of Delft*, in the Mauritshuis, with the town you see today. At the Markt, the splendid 17th-century **Waag** was designed by Hendrick de Keyser. The **Nieuwe Kerk**, built at the end of the 14th century, contains the magnificent de Keyser tomb of William of Orange.
• 60 km southwest; trains leave on average twice an hour and take 50 min direct from Centraal Station. Touristen Informatie Punt Hippolytusbuurt 4 ☎ 0900 515 15 55.

The Hague (maps 1, 4) Den Haag is the seat of government, home to the International Court of Justice and favoured residence of Queen Beatrix. Parliament sits in the **Binnenhof**, a Gothic castle that contains the 13th-century Knights' Hall, Ridderzaal. The **Mauritshuis**, one of Europe's greatest art galleries, set in a 17th-century mansion, has works by all the Dutch Masters, including Rembrandt's *Anatomy Lesson of Dr Tulp* and Vermeer's *View of Delft* and *Girl with the Pearl Earring*. Tram No. 10 takes you to the **Gemeentemuseum**, with paintings by Picasso, Braque and the largest collection of Mondrian in the world. Trams 1, 7, and 9 go to **Scheveningen**, a seaside resort. Don't miss the **Kurhaus**, a spa hotel and casino dating from 1887. • 50 km southwest; trains leave on average four times an hour from Centraal Station and take 50 min to Den Haag Centraal Spoor. VVV Den Haag, Spui 68 ☎ 0900 340 35 05

Rotterdam (maps 1, 5) Located on the mouth of the River Maas, Rotterdam is the No. 1 port of the world, so it's well worth spending a couple of hours on a commercial harbour cruise to let its sheer size sink in. The first installations were built in the 16th century, and as the tonnage of the ships increased, adaptations were required in the form of new canals, channels and facilities. In World War II most of the port and the old town were destroyed. Everything had to be rebuilt from scratch, and the modern high-rise city that emerged from the ashes more than merits its nickname of "Manhattan on the Maas". In summer, the "tourist hopper" double-decker bus takes you past the major attractions. With a day-ticket, you can hop on and off as often as you like. You may want to alight first at the **Euromast**, where you have a different kind of view of the port and city—from on high. The view from the tower at 100 m (328 ft) is grand enough, but the one in the round at 185 m (607 ft) will leave you speechless, especially at night with all the lights twinkling. There's a restaurant at the top.

The leaning cubic houses in Rotterdam, designed by Piet Blom.

Down on firm ground, wander into nearby **Museumpark**. The group of five museums cover a range of art and sculpture, architecture and navigation. Head first to the exceptional **Boymans-van Beuningen Museum**. An impressive collection of paintings, prints and drawings and decorative arts covers the 15th to the 20th centuries. The decorative arts collection with its silver and Persian and Turkish ceramics is outstanding. In the Leuvenhaven area is **Het Schielandshuis**, Rotterdam's history museum, and **Prins Hendrik Maritime Museum**. Boatlovers will also note the historic sailing vessels berthed in the **Oude Haven** and **Delfshaven** districts. In the latter quarter, some old warehouses set the scene for **De Dubbele Palmboom Museum**, which spells out the history of Rotterdam in photographs and models. Oude Haven, famous for its jolly nightlife, is fringed by architect Piet Blom's extraordinary cube houses, one of which, the **Kijk-Kubus**, is furnished and open for viewing. • 72 km (45 miles) south; trains take 1 hour direct from Centraal Station. VVV Rotterdam, Coolsingel 195 ☎ 010 271 01 20.

cityBites

Amsterdammers' tastebuds have been permanently internationalized by their history. French cuisine has been enormously popular since the time of Napoleonic rule, but it is Holland's colonial past that has left the deepest mark. This is the place to come for Indonesian food, and it would be a shame to leave without trying some. It is now so integral to eating here that the Dutch almost consider it their national cuisine. Also listed here are some of Amsterdam's best brown cafés, Grand Cafés and *eethuisjes*, which combine a great atmosphere with down-to-earth cuisine and prices to match. Bear in mind that the Dutch eat early—any time between 6pm and 9pm—and the kitchens may often close by 10pm. If you want to eat late, be sure to phone ahead and check that it's possible.

Prices are indicated as follows:

1 = reasonable (under 20 euros)
2 = medium (20–50 euros)
3 = expensive (over 50 euros)

CENTRAL AMSTERDAM

Café Bern
🚊 9, 14
Nieuwmarkt 9
☎ 020 622 00 34
Mon–Sun 6–11pm
[1]

Originally Swiss, and an institution in Amsterdam. The menu has remained the same seemingly for ever: cheese fondue, steak au poivre, entrecôte Café Bern. Popular with locals.

De Blauwe Parade
🚊 1, 2, 5, 13, 17
Nieuwezijds Voorburgwal 176–180
☎ 020 714 20 00
Daily noon–midnight
[2]

Situated in the Hotel Port van Cleve, this former 19th-century beer hall offers excellent Dutch food, with steaks a speciality. The restaurant's name comes from the decoration of old Delft Blue tiles.

De Doelen
🚊 4, 9, 14
Kloveniersburgwal 125
☎ 020 624 90 23
[1]

An eclectic mix of clientele makes for a lively atmosphere in this café.

De Jaren, with its pleasant waterside terrace.

De Jaren
🚊 4, 9, 14, 16, 24, 25
Nieuwe Doelenstraat 20
☎ 020 625 57 71
[2]

Bright, cheerful Grand Café in a nicely renovated old building by the Amstel river, with a waterside terrace. Theatre café that attracts a large arty crowd from nearby venues. Also has good food available in a relaxed atmosphere.

Flo Amsterdam
🚊 4, 9, 14
Amstelstraat 9 (in Eden Rembrandt Square Hotel)
☎ 020 890 47 57
Daily 5.30pm–midnight. Lunch Mon–Fri, noon–3pm
[2]

The classic French brasserie has been a hit ever since it landed in Amsterdam.

t'Gasthuis
🚊 4, 9, 14, 16, 24, 25
Grimburgwal 7
☎ 020 624 82 30
[1]

A lively student bar near the university—but with a fairly peaceful canalside terrace at the front.

The Grand
🚊 9, 14, 16, 24, 25
Sofitel Hotel
Oudezijds Voorburgwal 197
☎ 020 555 32 82
Daily 6.30am–11pm
[2] [3]

Authentic French cuisine supervised by chef Aurélien Poirot; award-winning wine list.

Kantjil en de Tijger
🚊 1, 2, 5
Spuistraat 291–293
☎ 020 620 09 94
Daily 4.30–11pm
[2] [3]

Very good, authentic Indonesian food in a large, stylish restaurant.

Keuken van 1870
🚇 1, 2, 5
Spuistraat 4
☎ 020 620 40 18
Mon–Sat 5–10pm
[1]

This restaurant began as a soup kitchen in 1870 and retains a lively, communal atmosphere. Cheap, earthy meals of *stamppot*, sausages etc., piled high on the plate.

Café Luxembourg
🚇 1, 2, 5
Spui 24
☎ 020 620 62 64
[2]

Very much the place to go if you want to be with the smart set. An elegant grand café whose snacks are widely acclaimed for their quality (and quantity). Cosmopolitan atmosphere.

Oriental City
🚇 4, 9, 14, 16, 24, 25
Oudezijds Voorburgwal 177–179
☎ 020 626 83 52
Daily 11.30am–10.30pm
[1] [2]

A large Chinese and Indonesian restaurant near Dam Square. Excellent *dim sum*, encouragingly popular with the local Chinese community, especially at weekends.

De Silveren Spiegel
🚇 1, 2, 5, 13, 17
Kattengat 4–6
☎ 020 624 65 89
Mon–Sat 5.30pm–10.30pm
[2] [3]

Elegant French cuisine with a Dutch touch; the menu often features lamb, and game in season. The crooked, step-gabled building by Hendrick de Keyser dates from 1614. The delightful interior has the original Delft tiles and panelled walls. Book at least a day in advance.

Supperclub
🚇 1, 2, 9 13, 17, 24
Jonge Roelensteeg 21
☎ 020 344 64 00
Open from 8 pm. Book three to four weeks ahead by phone or on www.supperclub.nl
[3]

Decidedly different. For a cover charge of 60 euro, a 5-course surprise menu will be served to you, as you recline on a bed. They call it the "ultimate sensual experience"— anything can happen.

Theatercafé Blincker
🚇 4, 9, 14, 16, 24, 25
Sint Barberenstraat 7
☎ 020 627 19 38
Opens at 4pm
[1]

Friendly brown café serving snacks, salads, mixed grill, vegetarian dishes.

De Waag
🚇 Nieuwmarkt
Nieuwmarkt 4
☎ 020 422 77 72
Daily 10am–10.30pm. Dinner 5pm–10.30pm
[2]

Great setting for Franco-Dutch style food in one of the city's most famous medieval buildings.

JORDAAN AND WESTERN GRACHTENGORDEL

Belhamel
🚇 1, 2, 5, 13, 17
Brouwersgracht 60
☎ 020 622 10 95
Mon–Fri 6–10pm
Sat, Sun 6–10.30pm
[2]

Good French food in a fine Art Nouveau interior, by one of Amsterdam's prettiest canals.

Cilubang
🚇 1, 2, 5, 11
Runstraat 10
☎ 020 626 9755
Tues–Sun from 6pm
[2]

The friendly owners are from West Java and serve delicious Indonesian food with a beautifully decorated and very cosy interior.

Café Nol
🚋 10
Westerstraat 109
☎ 020 624 53 80
Mon, Wed, Thurs, Sun 9pm–3am;
Fri, Sat 9pm–4am
①

Raucous Jordaan bar which manages to capture the flavour of the whole area with its slightly kitsch interior.

Thijssen
🚋 3
Brouwersgracht 107
☎ 020 623 89 94
①

A Jordaan bar with good brunches and a very laid-back atmosphere, helped by its pleasant location and views of the canal.

Toscanini Caffè
🚋 3, 10
Lindengracht 75
☎ 020 623 28 13
Mon–Sat 6–10.30pm
① ②

Excellent Italian food, with a lot more than pasta on the menu.

De Tuin
🚋 3, 10
Tweede Tuindwarsstraat 13
☎ 020 624 45 59
①

A typical Jordaan café, with a stone floor and large tables occupied by locals lingering over their drinks and enjoying the eternal pleasures of newspaper-reading, chess-playing and conversation.

De Vliegende Schotel
🚋 13, 14, 17
Nieuwe Leliestraat 162
☎ 020 625 20 41
Daily 4–10.45pm
①

Good-sized helpings of tasty vegetarian food make this laid-back restaurant popular with locals.

't Zwaantje
🚋 13, 14, 17
Berenstraat 12
☎ 020 623 23 73
Open 4.30–11pm
① ②

Vast portions of traditional Dutch food to satisfy the biggest appetite.

SOUTHERN GRACHTENGORDEL AND THE AMSTEL

Huyschkaemer
🚋 4
Utrechtsestraat 137
☎ 020 627 05 75
Opens at 3.30pm
①

Trendy bar and restaurant with post-industrial kitsch decor, frequented by the gay community.

De Kroon
🚋 4, 9, 14
Rembrandtplein 17/1
☎ 020 625 20 11
Sun–Thurs 10.30am–1am, Fri, Sat 10.30am–3am
① ②

Designed in colonial style, the café is on the first floor and has a great view over Rembrandtplein. It first opened in 1898 and was named in honour of Queen Wilhelmina's coronation, which took place the same year.

Moko
🚋 4, 6, 7, 10
Amstelveld 12
☎ 020 626 11 99
Tues–Sun noon–3am
① ②

Pleasantly located on a traffic-free square, the restaurant is chic and modern, with lots of bamboo and leather, and fish tanks along the walls. The food is defined as "free-style". Music and dancing Friday nights with a DJ. Great terrace.

Het Molenpad
🚋 1, 2, 5, 7, 10

CITYBITES

Prinsengracht 653
☎ 020 625 96 80
Opens at noon
1
Frequented by an art gallery crowd, this typical brown café is known for its food and the pictures on its walls (changing exhibitions).

L'Opera
T 4, 9, 14
Rembrandtplein 27–29
☎ 020 620 47 54
1 2
Lively café in elegant French Art Deco style, with a terrace for great people-watching.

Rose's Cantina
T 4, 9, 14, 16, 24, 25
Reguliersdwarsstraat 38–40
☎ 020 625 97 97
Daily 5–11.30pm
Fri, Sat till 11pm. Bar open weekends till 2am
1
Tasty Mexican food in a boisterous restaurant.

Café Schiller
T 4, 9, 14
Rembrandtplein 24
☎ 020 624 98 46
Opens at 4pm
1 2
A celebrated Art Deco café attached to the Schiller Hotel. It has

GOING DUTCH

Indonesian cuisine is as popular in Amsterdam as chicken tikka masala is in London. While you're there be sure to sample the famous *rijsttafel*, a highly sociable meal served for two or more and consisting of masses of spicy sweet and sour dishes eaten with plain rice. However, Dutch cooking should not be written off entirely. The traditional restaurant's friendly atmosphere and hearty portions of *erwtensoep* (a thick pea and ham soup), *stamppot* (meat and vegetable mash), or *boerenkool met rookworst* (kale and potatoes with smoked sausage), should keep you filled up for the whole day. And if you're in too much of a hurry for this you can always be like the locals and stop at one of the fish kiosks around town, such as the Vishuisje Herengracht by the bridge where Herengracht meets Utrechtsestraat. Here you can snack on fresh raw herring or, as some Amsterdammers like to call it, "Dutch sushi".

become an institution among Amsterdam's café-going and theatre crowd, who come here for pre-show meals.

Sluizer Restaurants
☎ 4
Utrechtsestraat 41–43–45
☏ 020 622 63 76
Daily 5–11pm;
Fri, Sat till midnight
Lunch on request
2

The famous fish restaurant at No. 45 has extended its bill of fare to include meat, which is served in a separate restaurant, next door.

Tempo Doeloe
☎ 4
Utrechtsestraat 75
☏ 020 625 67 18
Daily 6–11.30pm
Reservation only
2

A beautifully designed restaurant, offering some of the best Indonesian food in Amsterdam.

Zuid Zeeland
☎ 4, 9, 14, 16, 24, 25
Herengracht 413
☏ 020 624 31 54
Lunch Mon–Fri noon–2.30pm
Dinner daily 6–11pm
2 3

A sophisticated restaurant with a slant towards fish dishes, in a quiet area.

PLANTAGEBUURT AND DOCKLANDS

Plancius
☎ 7, 9, 14
Plantage Kerklaan 61a
☏ 020 330 94 69
Daily 11am–11pm; Sat, Sun breakfast from 10am
1 2

Feeding time is always fun at this stylish restaurant opposite Artis Zoo, but the lunches are specially worthy of a lion-size appetite.

Star Ferry
☎ 25
Piet Heinkade 1
☏ 020 788 2090
Lunch 11am–3.30pm, dinner 5.30–10pm
1 2

Housed in the cool Muziekgebouw Aan 't IJ, this café-restaurant by the riverside is equally good for afternoon coffee and cake or pre- and post-concert dinner.

A Tavola
Ⓑ 22, 43
Kadijksplein 9
☏ 020 625 4994
Mon–Sat 6am–10.30pm
1

Superb Italian restaurant near the Entrepotdok, with pasta dishes guaranteed to keep landlubbers well and truly satisfied.

Café Américain

MUSEUMBUURT AND LEIDSEPLEIN

Café Américain
☎ 1, 2, 5, 6, 7, 10
Leidsekade 97
☏ 020 556 30 00
Daily 7am–11pm
1

Café and brasserie in an Art Nouveau setting dating from 1902, with stained-glass windows.

De Blauwe Hollander
☎ 6, 7, 10
Leidsekruisstraat 28
☏ 020 627 05 21
Daily noon–11pm
1 2

Tasty and traditional Dutch fare in cosy surroundings. Good value.

Bodega Keyzer
☎ 2, 3, 5, 12, 16
Van Baerlestraat 96
☏ 020 675 18 66

Mon–Sat 9am–midnight,
Sun 11am–midnight
2 3
Stylish, French-influenced eating spot next to the Concertgebouw. It counts famous conductors and performers among its clientele.

Bojo
1, 2, 5
Lange Leidsedwarsstraat 51
☎ 020 622 74 34
Mon–Fri 11am–9pm;
Sat, Sun 4.30pm–9pm
1

Small Indonesian restaurant, with wide range of dishes and good vegetarian food.

Le Garage
3, 5, 6, 12, 16
Ruysdaelstraat 54
☎ 020 679 71 76
Mon–Fri lunch noon–2 pm, dinner 6–11pm
2

Expensive, top-quality "fusion food". The haunt of TV celebrities, a place to see and be seen—and it's quite dressy. The venue is a 1950s garage.

Puri Mas
1, 2, 5
Lange Leidsedwarsstraat 37–41
☎ 020627 76 27
Daily 5pm–11pm
1 2

Excellent Indonesian cuisine in pleasant surroundings. One of the best places for sampling the *rijsttafel*.

De Smoeshaan Theatercafé
1, 2, 5, 6, 7, 10, 11
Leidsekade 90
☎ 020 625 03 68
Café daily 11am–1am;
Sat, Sun till 3am;
lunch 11.30am–4 pm, dinner 5.30pm –9pm
1

A downstairs café and upstairs restaurant, both of them popular with actors and theatre-goers in the Leidseplein area.

Café Vertigo
1, 3, 6, 12
Vondelpark 3
☎ 020 612 30 21
Daily 11am–1am
Sat, Sun 10am–1am
1

Located in a 19th-century pavilion overlooking Vondelpark, it matches the menu to the films showing upstairs in the Nederlands Filmmuseum.

DE PIJP AND OOSTERPARKBUURT

Albert Cuyp 67
16, 24
Albert Cuypstraat 67
☎ 020 671 13 96
1

A Chinese-Surinamese hybrid. Their *roti kip*, a chicken curry with vegetables and a large roti bread, is a lynchpin of Surinamese cuisine and an incredibly inexpensive hunger-buster.

Le Hollandais
3, 4
Amsteldijk 41
☎ 020 679 12 48
Tues–Sat 6pm–10.30pm
2

Modern, French cuisine with all the accents in the right place: on the food itself.

Klokspijs
4, 7, 10, 25
Hemonystraat 38
☎ 020 364 25 60
Tues–Sat 5.45–10pm
2

Excellent unpretentious cuisine in an old bellmaker's workshop.

WESTERPARK AMSTERDAM WEST

Amsterdam
10
Watertorenplein 6
☎ 020 682 25 66
Sun–Thurs 10.30am–midnight
Fri–Sat 10.30am–1am
1

Huge café-restaurant in a converted pumping plant. Good, classic food.

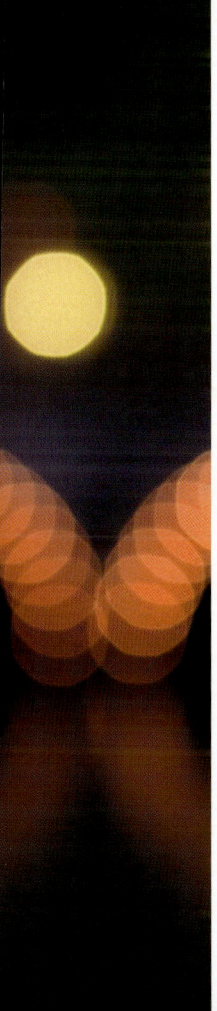

cityNights

To find out what's on, ask at one of the three VVV tourist information offices: Stationsplein 10 (opposite the railway station), Stadhouderskade 550 (opposite No. 78) and in the Muziektheater, Amstel 3), or the AUB Ticketshop (Leidseplein 26), on the terrace side. You can also consult the *What's on in Amsterdam* magazine in English, or the listings paper *Uitkrant* in Dutch. Tickets can be bought through the AUB Uitburo, or at the box office. From September to June, many venues have free lunchtime concerts.

LATE NIGHT SHOPPING

Most shops in Amsterdam close fairly early. But if it's past midnight and you find you've run out of toothpaste or fancy a bottle of wine, there are places that will see you through the night.

Dolf's Avondverkoop

(Willemsstraat 79) is a general purpose store in Jordaan that opens every night of the week till 1am and sells bread, juice and, yes, toothpaste.

De Avondmarkt

(De Wittekade 94) is the biggest in Amsterdam and sells almost everything. Open from 4pm till midnight.

On Waterlooplein, **Sterk** (Waterlooplein 241), open till 2am, will satisfy witching hour desires for fruit, pastries, vegetables and wine.

MAJOR ARTS VENUES

Beurs van Berlage
🚋 4, 9, 16, 24, 25
Damrak 213
☎ 020 530 41 41

Also exhibitions, congresses and various events. There are two concert halls in the old stock exchange, the Yakult Zaal and the smaller Amvest Zaal, where you can listen to recitals by famous orchestras, but also soloists and more varied music such as tango festivals.

Boom Chicago
🚋 1, 2, 5, 7, 10
Leidseplein 12
☎ 020 423 01 01
Lunch Mon–Sat noon–4 pm
Dinner daily 6–9 pm

Political comedy theatre in English about Amsterdam, the Netherlands and the rest of the world.

Concertgebouw
🚋 2, 3, 5, 12, 16
Concertgebouwplein 2–6
☎ 020 671 83 45

With its world-class Royal Concertgebouw Orchestra and heavenly acoustics, this concert hall is an absolute must for the classical music fan. It may be best to reserve your concert tickets in advance. The Small Hall (Kleine Zaal), reserved for chamber works, offers free lunchtime recitals on Wednesdays at 12.30pm.

Koninklijk Theater Carré
🚋 4, 6, 7, 10
Amstel 115–125
☎ 0900 252 52 55

Built in 1887 as a circus, this is now a venue for big international musicals such as the Lloyd-Webber operas, and other touring extravaganzas.

Muziekgebouw aan 't IJ
🚋 1, 2, 4, 5, 9, 13, 16, 17, 24, 25
Piet Heinkade 1
☎ 020 788 20 00
Ticket sales Mon–Sat noon –6 p.m.
For events and concerts see:
www.muziekgebouw.nl, www.bimhuis.nl

The spectacular new building on the waterfront proposes an adventurous programme of contemporary chamber and experimental music, often with short seasons dedicated to one specific modern composer or a specific instrument. Performances are guaranteed to challenge your musical preconceptions. The

Muziekgebouw incorporates the Bimhuis, Amsterdam's premier jazz venue, mixing major names from overseas with home-grown talent. A must for the serious jazz fan.

Muziektheater (Stopera)
🚋 4, 9, 14
Ⓜ Waterlooplein
Waterlooplein 22
☎ 020 625 54 55
The building's post-modern design caused protests and riots prior to its opening in 1986, so it's worth seeing what all the fuss was about. Some critics find that the acoustics leave a little to be desired, but the theatre is home to the National Ballet and the Netherlands Opera and offers large-scale performances at reasonable prices. Free lunchtime concert on Tuesday at 12.30pm.

Stadsschouwburg
🚋 1, 2, 5, 6, 7, 10
Leidseplein 26
☎ 020 624 23 11
A fine old theatre in the heart of the Leidseplein area, with performances of opera, dance and drama, including occasional productions in English.

Peep into the lobby of the Theater Tuschinski.

Studio K
🚋 14
Timorplein 62
☎ 020 69 20 422
Sun–Thurs 11am–1am
Fri–Sat 11–3 or 4am
Old school building used for film, theatre, music, art exhibitions and café and restaurant. Popular and interesting.

Theater Tuschinski
🚋 4, 9, 10
Reguliersbreestraat 26
☎ 0900 235 72 84
Guided tours for groups of at least 15: www.cultuurinvoorraad.nl
One of the most lavishly decorated cinemas in the world, incorporating elements of Art Deco and Art Nouveau, paintings, exotic woods, marble, stained glass, splendid chandeliers, bas-reliefs and sculpture. The Wurlitzer pipe organ, which accompanied silent movies in the 20s, is now used for concerts.

Cultuurpark Westergasfabriek
🚋 10
Poloneeankade 27
☎ 020 586 07 10
Ketelhuis Cinema:
☎ 020 684 00 90
An obsolete gasworks, the Westergasfabriek has been transformed into a culture complex, linked with the pleasant Westerpark. It includes shops, restaurants and cafés, exhibition space and several galleries. The latest films are shown in the Ketelhuis Cinema, and you can dance till late at night in the Flex Bar. From early morning there's

fresh bread and fine coffee at the baker's shop and the Espresso Factory. The renovated buildings can be hired for various events, meetings and workshops: the Gasometer, the Transformatorhuis, the Zuiveringshal (Purification Hall), the Machinegebouw (Machine Building) and the Oostelijk Meterhuis (Eastern Meter House).

NIGHTCLUBS

Amsterdam has a thriving nightclub scene attracting people from around the world. The clubs are usually relaxed about dress; they open from around 10 pm–4am (although there's little point rushing to get there before midnight). It's considered good form to tip the bouncer a couple of euros on your way out.

Arena (Tonight)
🚃 3, 6, 7, 10
Gravesandestraat 51
☎ 020 850 24 30
A dance and live music club in the Arena hotel.

Escape
🚃 4, 9, 14
Rembrandtplein 11
☎ 020 622 11 11
The biggest disco in town, with a good sound system, lasers and videos. Very popular with tourists.

Odeon Club
🚃 1, 2, 5
Singel 460
☎ 020 521 85 55
Thurs–Sat from 11 p.m. Rebuilt after a fire, and re-opened in its present form in 2005, this pleasant club in a 17th-century brewery targets "mature and discerning tastes".

Odessa
🚌 28, 32, 39
Veemkade 259
☎ 020 311 86 86
A boat on the IJ that makes a trendy place for eating and dancing.

Panama
🚌 28, 32, 39
Oostelijke Handelskade 4
☎ 020 311 86 89
Popular with the 30s age group. Live music, rather expensive.

Toomler
🚃 5, 16, 24
Breitnerstraat 2
reserveringen@toomler.nl
Very popular nightclub with stand-up comedians, and sometimes live bands.

Winston International
🚃 1, 2, 4, 5, 9, 14
Warmoesstraat 129
☎ 020 623 13 80
Live bands play very danceable music for visitors and locals.

JAZZ AND ROCK VENUES

Alto Jazz Café
🚃 1, 2, 5, 6, 7, 10
Korte Leidsedwarsstraat 115
☎ 020 626 32 49
Close to the Leidseplein area, this jazz bar features top quality acts every night of the week, by in-house musicians and guests.

Bamboo Bar
🚃 1, 2, 5, 6, 7, 10
Lange Leidsedwarsstraat 70
☎ 020 7769614
A crowded bar with performances of blues and jazz, with occasional forays into world music.

Bourbon Street
🚃 1, 2, 5, 6, 7, 10
Leidsekruisstraat 6–8
☎ 020 623 34 40
Late-night blues café, with a suitably cool atmosphere.

De Heeren van Aemstel
🚃 4, 9, 14
Thorbeckeplein 5
☎ 020 620 21 73

There's good live music every night at this student haunt, and the chance of well-known guest musicians dropping in for the Sunday session.

Maloe Melo
🚊 7, 10
Lijnbaansgracht 163
☎ 020 420 45 92
Live performances of blues and rock every evening in this popular venue considered to be Amsterdam's House of the Blues. Relaxed atmosphere. Local and international bands.

Melkweg
🚊 1, 2, 5, 6, 7, 10
Lijnbaansgracht 234/A
☎ 020 531 81 81
This place was something of a legend in the 1960s and still going strong. The tradition continues with mainly British and American rock bands and music from Brazil to Zaire. Saturday night is dance night.

Paradiso
🚊 1, 2, 5, 6, 7, 10
Weteringschans 6–8
☎ 020 626 45 21
Since the 1960s this converted church has been host to some of the biggest names in rock music, and it remains a favourite venue for local bands.

THE RLD

Known informally by its initials, Amsterdam's Red Light District is notorious for the sex industry that flourishes there, although these days things are a bit more low key than in former years. It has been at the heart of the saltier side of life ever since sailors from ships moored in the Oosterdok used to frequent the bars and other places of entertainment along Zeedijk in the 17th century. Today however, it's not that seedy a place—things are far too open and casual for that. Indeed, you may be surprised by the crowds milling around the ancient streets—but this is because ultimately the RDL has developed into a famous tourist sight. If you want a walk on the wild side, it is a remarkable place with plenty to surprise even for the most cosmopolitan. Astonishingly, it is also pretty safe, if only because of the great throngs of people here day and night. Be prepared to experience something that is well and truly eye-opening.

cityFacts

Airport	98
Babysitting	98
Canal Tours	98
Climate	98
Communications	98
Customs and Entry Formalities	99
Cycling	99
Disabled	100
Driving	100
Drugs	101
Electricity	101
Emergencies	101
Lost and Found	101
Money Matters	101
Public Holidays	102
Public Transport	102
Safety Precautions	105
Time	105
Tipping	105
Toilets	105
Tourist Information Offices	105

Airport

Schiphol Airport is 15 km southwest of Amsterdam. For general airport information call:

☎ 0900 01 41

Trains leave for Centraal Station every 15 minutes between 4am and midnight, and hourly during the night. The journey takes 20 minutes. Connexxion Schiphol Hotel Shuttle brings airline passengers to more than 100 hotels between 6am and 9pm. It leaves every 10 minutes from stop A7 near Aankomsthal. Tickets available at the Connexxion desk, hotels and VVV:

☎ 020 201 88 00

A taxi from Schiphol to the centre of Amsterdam will cost around €40 (more at night).

Babysitting

The larger hotels may have their own child-minding facilities. Babysitters are listed in the phone book under Oppascentrales.

Canal Tours

Tours usually take one hour; they have multilingual commentaries. The majority leave from Damrak, outside Centraal Station, and the operators all offer pretty much the same tour. About 20 per cent of the boats are electronically powered, which avoids engine noise.

Climate

Amsterdam's weather is very changeable, though generally temperate. It might be wet or sunny in summer or winter, and is as likely to be both on the same day. Summers are rarely hot, winters mild, and all year round there can be a bitingly cold wind blowing in from the North Sea. Average temperatures are 16–19°C (61–67°F) in summer, and 4–6°C (39–42°F) in winter.

Communications

Telephone. The area code for Amsterdam is 020. To telephone abroad from Amsterdam, dial 00 + country code (UK 44, USA and Canada 1) + area code (without 0) + number. You can make international calls from public phone boxes; all instructions are in English and Dutch. Off-peak rates are from 8pm–8am, and at weekends. Most phone boxes now use only phonecards, available from post offices and phone centres.

The Netherlands uses the GSM mobile phone system. To save roaming charges you can buy a pre-paid SIM card to use in your own phone, or, if you only want to use it in the Netherlands, you could purchase an inexpensive phone with a pre-paid calling plan in supermarkets or phone stores.

Useful numbers
Directory Enquiries: ☎ 1888
International Operator and Directory: ☎ 1800
Collect calls abroad: ☎ 1 800 225 5453

Post offices are normally open Mon–Fri 9am–5pm, and the main offices also open Saturday 9am–noon. Stamps are also sold at many tobacconists, supermarkets and souvenir shops.

Customs and Entry Formalities
Nationals of the EU countries, the US, Canada, Australia and New Zealand need only a valid passport to enter the Netherlands. For more information, contact your nearest Dutch Embassy or Consulate. Following the Schengen agreement of 1995, it should be possible to enter the country from within the EU without documentation checks, but it is wise to have your passport ready. The allowance for duty-free importation of goods (for those over the age of 17) is 200 cigarettes or 50 cigars or 250 g of tobacco, 1 litre of spirits, 5 litres of wine (2 litres for non-EU residents). In theory, there is no limit on the amount of duty-paid goods for personal consumption carried within the EU.

Cycling
Amsterdam is perfect for the would-be cyclist—it's flat, covered in cycle lanes, and filled with hire shops. At Centraal Station there is MacBike:
☎ 020 624 83 91
while in the Beurs van Berlage basement you'll find Holland Rent-a-Bike:
☎ 020 622 32 07

Be prepared to leave a hefty deposit. For a 3-hour cycle tour try Mike's Bike Tours Amsterdam, Kerkstraat 134, March– Nov daily 9am–4pm; Dec–Feb 10am–noon:

☎ 020 622 79 70

Always lock your cycle, and watch out for your fellow pedallers—there's a lot of them, and they tend to ignore the rules.

Disabled

The major museums, concert halls, churches, public buildings and the metro have been modified to make them accessible to visitors in wheelchairs. Trams are still very difficult to board, however. Disabled persons needing assistance with taxis should call one of the following numbers:

☎ 020 696 96 40
☎ 020 691 05 18
☎ 020 615 718 88
☎ 020 584 0100
☎ 020 663 48 11

Netherlands Railways has timetables in Braille, a useful information booklet, and offers assistance at the station. For details call:

☎ 020 235 78 22

If you require more general advice on life in Amsterdam for the disabled, call the MEE Amstel en Zaan:

☎ 020 512 72 72.

Driving

Driving in Amsterdam comes with a big warning: the authorities don't want cars in their city, and if you park illegally you will be fined heavily. A white note on the windscreen will explain how to pay the fine. If you park somewhere very inconvenient your car will be towed away. Almost the whole city centre is metered: Mon–Sat 9am–11pm, Sun noon–11pm. Luckily, your hotel can sell you parking cards valid for one or three days. Meters cost up to €3 per hour, which becomes expensive over a whole day. In town, trams have priority, so keep out of their way, and always beware of cyclists.

If you need a car for touring, the best solution might be to hire one when you're in Amsterdam. You'll need a valid driver's licence, a credit card for

the deposit, and you will probably have to be over 21. The Dutch drive on the right; seatbelts are compulsory for all passengers. Speed limits are 50 kph in town, 80 kph outside, and 120 kph on motorways. The Dutch motoring club, the ANWB, has a 24-hour emergency line:
 ☎ 088 269 28 88.

Drugs
Despite its reputation, Amsterdam is not a haven for drugs. The authorities tolerate soft drugs, like cannabis, in small quantities of up to 30g, and for personal use only. Trafficking is illegal and people should be careful where they buy it and where they use it. Production, trading and stocking drugs remain a criminal offence. Driving under the influence of soft drugs is penalized in the same way as driving under the influence of alcohol.

Electricity
The current is 220 volts AC, 50 Hz, for plugs with two round pins. British and American equipment requires an adaptor.

Emergencies
General emergency number: ☎ 112
Police: ☎ 0900 88 44
Fire: ☎ 621 21 21
Health advice, Tourist Medical Service: ☎ 020 592 33 55
Dental patient information bureau: ☎ 020 518 82 04
The Farmaceutisch bureau Amsterdam gives information about chemists:
 ☎ 020 624 30 79
and information for after-hour chemists between 11pm and 8.30am:
 ☎ 020 510 88 26.
The following hospitals have a 24-hour outpatients department
Academisch Medisch Centrum, Meibergdreef 9: ☎ 020 566 91 11
Onze Lieve Vrouwe Gasthuis, Eerste Oosterparkstraat: ☎ 020 599 91 11
VU hospital, De Boelelaan 1118: ☎ 020 444 36 36
EU nationals are entitled to use Dutch medical services, as long as they hold a European Health Card. Non-EU nationals should take out health insurance prior to their trip.

Lost and Found

For property lost on a train or at the rail station, contact Centraal Station, NS Lost Property Information, Stationsplein 15, daily 8am–8pm:
☎ 0900 321 21 00

If you lose something on a bus, tram or metro, ask at the GVB head office (Klantenservice), Prins Hendrikkade 108–114, Monday to Friday 8am–7pm:
☎ 0900 80 11

For objects lost elsewhere in the city, call Police Lost Property, Korte Leidsedwarsstraat 52, Monday to Friday noon–4pm:
☎ 020 251 02 22

If you don't recover the property and you wish to make an insurance claim, you will need to have notified the police.

Money Matters

Banks generally open Monday to Friday 9am to 4 or 5pm, with some open later on Thursday. You can draw cash with cards such as Visa and Mastercard at most ATM machines using your NIP code. Exchange bureaux are usually open weekends as well, with a 24-hour bureau at Centraal Station.

Credit cards are accepted at all major hotels, and most restaurants and shops.

Currency. The Euro, divided into 100 cents. Coins from 1 to 50 cents, 1 and 2 euros; banknotes from 5 to 500 euros.

Public Holidays

January 1	New Year's Day
April 30	Queen's Birthday
December 25	Christmas Day
December 26	Boxing Day

Movable dates: Good Friday, Easter Monday, Ascension Day, Whit Monday

Public Transport

Canal bus. The boats from Canal Bus keep a regular service along three routes with 14 stops through the canals of Amsterdam. They stop at the important museums, attractions and shopping areas.

Trams and buses. Amsterdam's distinctive white trams are a great way to get about the city. Together with bus and metro, they constitute an impressively efficient, reliable and speedy public transport system.

You can obtain a Tourist Guide to Public Transport, which contains a map of tram, bus and metro routes, at the GVB (Municipal Transport Authority) office at Stationsplein 15. There are usually maps of the network in tram and bus shelters and on board the vehicles. Most drivers speak sufficient English to be able to give directions. Trams and buses run from 6am to around midnight on weekdays, and start at 6.30am on Saturday, and 7.30am on Sunday. After midnight, a night bus service takes over, with bus nos. 73 and 76 running through central Amsterdam. Night bus stops have a black square with the bus number on it.

Metro. The metro has four lines and is mainly a commuter service taking people to and from the suburbs. The trains start at 6am and run until 00.30am on weekdays, and start at 6.30am on Saturday and 7.30am on Sunday. All lines terminate at Centraal Station.

Tickets. The GVB network has introduced a series of smart cards for public transport. Visitors can purchase a **D-card** (Disposable OV-chipkaart) valid for 1 hour, 1 hour with a bicycle supplement, or 24, 48, 72, 96, 120, 144, 168 hours (i.e. 1 to 7 days, prices from €7 to €30). You have to check in and check out with your card at the beginning and end of every ride (including if you are changing vehicles). You can buy it from machines at underground stations or the GVB Tickets & Info service points, as well as from some tobacconists. People staying for longer periods, or residents, can obtain a **P-card** (Personal OV-chipkaart). It is valid for 5 years and costs €7.50. It bears a photo of the owner and has to be applied for in writing or online (the application form is in Dutch). It is reloadable and can be blocked in case of theft. The **A-card** (Anonymous OV-chipkaart), €7.50 and reloadable, can be used by different people but not simultaneously, and it cannot be blocked. The balance on these cards is automatically reset when you check out. The fare is calculated by distance travelled.

Fares are reduced for children from 4 to 11 and people aged 65 or older. For more information see www.gvb.nl.

The **All Amsterdam Transport Pass** includes a GVB one-day ticket, plus a one-day ticket for the Canalbus and discounts at museums, tourist attractions, restaurants and other facilities. Price €28, available at GVB Tickets & Info on Stationsplein and the Canalbus offices on Prins Hendrikkade. Canalbus ☎ +31 20 623 9886 www.canal.nl

The **I amsterdam Card** offers unlimited travel on all GVB tram, bus and metro services for up to three days, plus vouchers providing discounts on canal cruises, museums and other attractions. 1-day €39, 2-day €49, 3-day €59. Not valid in Connexxion, Arriva or BBA buses or NS trains.

Netherlands Railways. Dutch trains are clean, safe and punctual, with an extensive network and relatively good value. They are frequent, so reservations aren't necessary. From Amsterdam's Centraal Station you can get trains to most major towns throughout Europe. Reservations for international trains should be made in advance; The Dutch Railway Company NS has a website in English, where you can also book on line.

If you are travelling around the Netherlands, ask about the various rail passes available. There are day travel cards for 1 and 5 days. InterRail One Country passes, for European residents, are valid from three to eight days within a one-month period and cover Belgium, the Netherlands and Luxembourg. The InterRail Global Pass allows European travellers to use trains in 30 European countries.

For current train times, ticket offers and prices, go to www.ns.nl which also has a website in English, or call
Centraal Station Information Desk: ☎ 0900 92 92
NS Service: ☎ 0900 20 21 163, Mon–Fri 8am–6pm

Taxis. Amsterdam's taxis are a fairly expensive option for getting around town. The running charge should be displayed on the meter when you get in, and you will pay per kilometre on top, at a higher rate after midnight. The taxi stand at Centraal Station is regulated, and can only be used by taxis with a seal of approval. All taxis have an onboard computer to print out a receipt for the customer. You are not meant to hail a cab, but pick one up from a taxi rank, or by phoning the TCA central office:
☎ 020 677 77 77

Safety Precautions
Only carry the money you will need for the day along with a credit card. Deposit passports, plane tickets and any other valuables in the hotel safe if possible. Be careful where you put your wallets and purses as there is always the risk of pickpocketing in crowded places—and keep an eye on your bags in restaurants (do not leave them on the floor). Avoid isolated backstreets in the red-light district late at night. Give a wide berth to drug dealers and other insalubrious types, and they will leave you alone.

Time
Amsterdam follows UTC/GMT + 1, with summer time UTC/GMT + 2.

Tipping
By law, all hotel, restaurant, bar and café bills include a 15 per cent service charge. Amsterdammers tend to leave additional small change, but there's no obligation to do so. It is customary to tip porters and doormen at least 1 euro, and to round up taxi fares.

Toilets
Make use of toilets in museums, galleries, restaurants and cafés when possible. If you need one urgently, make for a department store, bar or café. If there is an attendant on duty, drop a coin in the dish on the way out. Toilets will usually be marked D or Dames for women, and H or Heren for men.

Tourist Information Offices (VVV)
The national tourist offices give general information about the city and the surrounding areas, plus specific help on hotel bookings, travel and tour arrangements, museums, galleries, concerts etc. The main VVV is outside Centraal Station: Stationsplein 10, Sun–Thurs 9am–5pm, Fri, Sat 9am–6pm. The office at Schiphol opens daily 7am–10pm, the one in the Muziektheater Mon–Fri noon–6pm, Sat, Sun noon–3pm; at Stadhouderskade 550 daily 9am–6pm. GAYtic at Spuistraat (for gay visitors) opens Mon–Sat 11am–8pm, Sun noon–8pm. ☎ 0900 400 40 40, www.iamsterdam.com For information and bookings for concerts and other cultural events, see the Leidseplein AUB Ticketshop, www.uitburo.nl

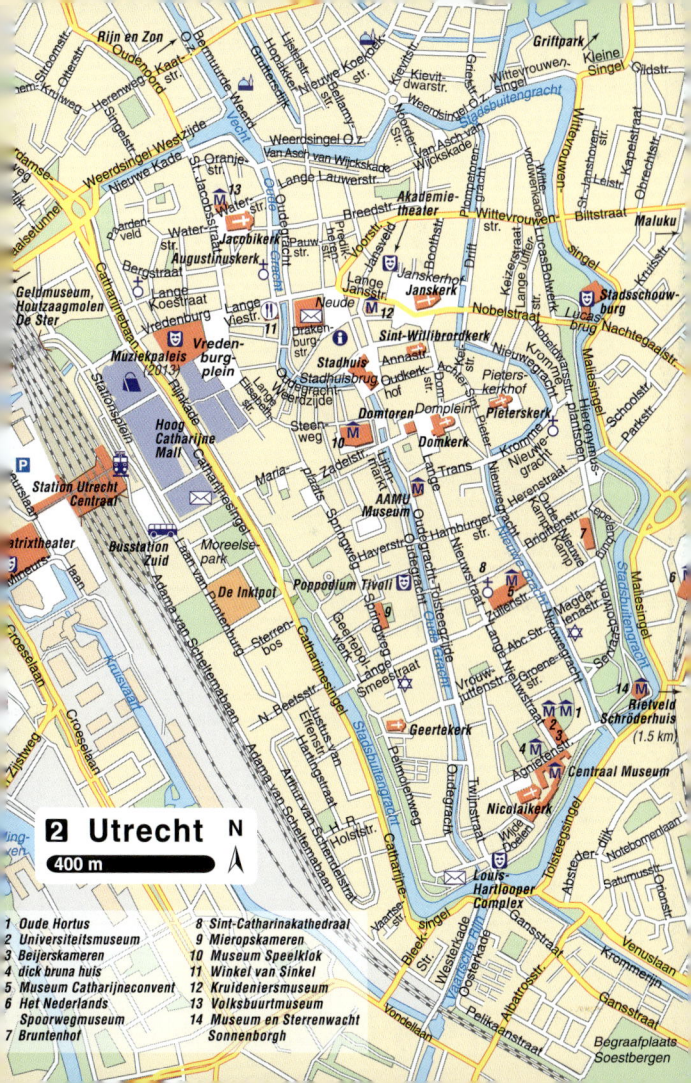

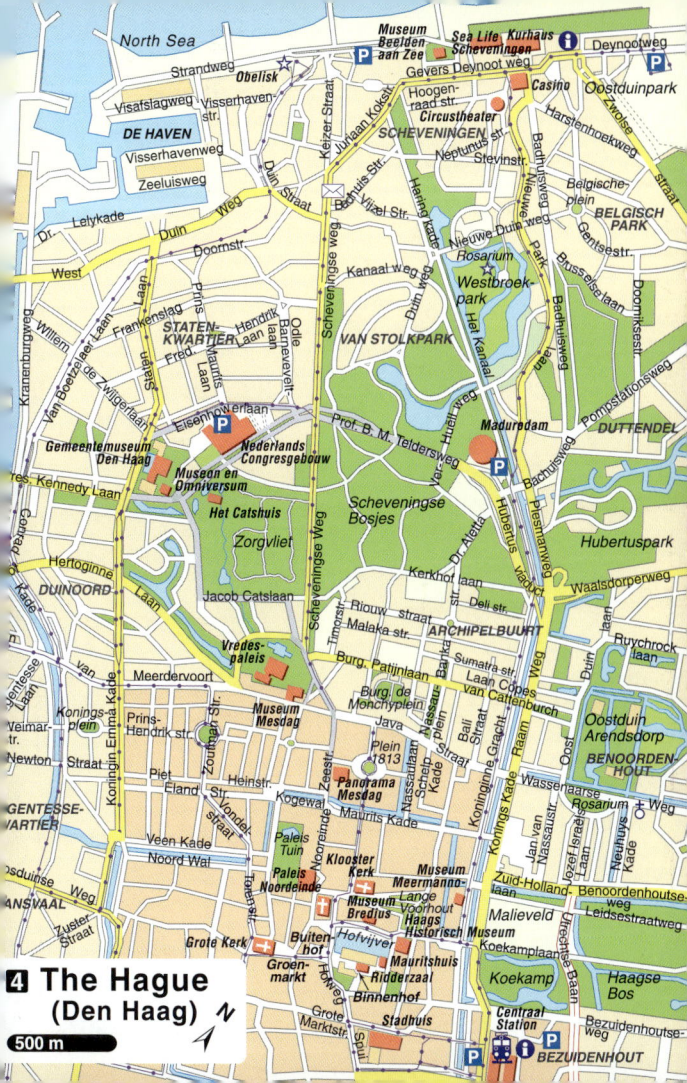

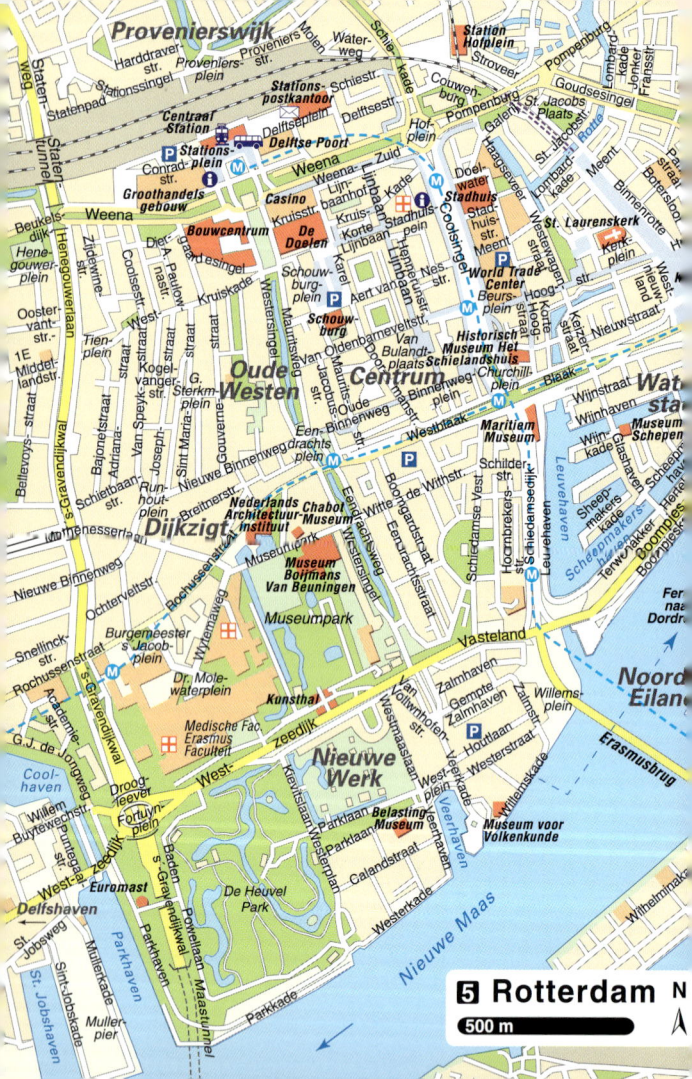

INDEX

Ajax Museum 57
Albert Cuypstraat 48, 70
Allard Pierson
 Museum 27, 30
Amstelhaven café 70
Amstelpark 56–57
Amsterdam Museum 23
 – School 17
 – Tulip Museum 34
Amsterdamse Bos 14, 57
Anne Frank Huis 34, 57
ARCAM 52
Artis Zoo 51, 54, 57
Begijnhof 26–27, 30
Beurs van Berlage 21, 92
Bijbels Museum 35
Blauwbrug 46
Bloemenmarkt 46, 49
Bloemgracht 36
Boom Chicago 92
Café Américain 39, 88
 – Dantzig 39
 – Hoppe 38
 – Luxembourg 39, 85
 – Vertigo 39, 64, 89
Cafés 38–39
Canal houses 32–33
Centraal Station 20–21
CoBrA Museum voor
 Moderne Kunst 57,
 63
Coffee shops 38
Concertgebouw 64, 92
Cultuurpark Westergas-
 fabriek 93–94
Dageraad 70
Dam Square 22, 30
De Bijenkorf 23
 – Drie Fleschjes 39
 – Druif 38
 – Linnenkist 30
 – Sluyswacht 46
Delft 79–80
Diamant Museum 61

Dockworker Statue 44
Dutch East India
 Building 27, 30
Eastern Islands 54
Elandsgracht 36
Entrepotdok 54
Felix Meritis Café 39
Flea market 46, 48
Flower market 46, 49
FOAM 42
Golden Bend 46
Grimburgwal 30
Haarlem 75–76
Heineken Experience
 68, 70
Herengracht 8, 33
Hermitage 51
Het Oranje Voetbal
 Museum 57
 – Scheepvaartmuseum
 52, 54
Hofjes 26
Hollandsche
 Schouwburg 52
Homomonument 36
Hortus Botanicus 50, 54
House of Bols 61–62, 64
IJburg 53
IJsselmeer 74–75
In 't Aepjen 30
Johnny Jordaanplein 36
Joods Historisch
 Museum 44
Kalverstraat 24, 30
Kattenkabinet 42, 46
Keizersgracht 8, 33
Keukenhof Bulb
 Gardens 79
Kleine Trippenhuis 30
Koninklijk Paleis 22
 – Theater Carré 92
L'Opera 39, 46, 87
Leiden 77–79
Leidseplein 63

Leidsestraat 24
Looier antiques
 market 49
Madame Tussauds
 Amsterdam 23
Magere Brug 43, 46
Magna Plaza 23
Markets 48–49
Mauritskade 70
Max Euwe Centrum 63
Montelbaanstoren 45
Mozes en Aäronkerk 44
Muiderpoort 70
Munttoren 30, 40–41
Museum Ons' Lieve
 Heer Op Solder 28
 – van Loon 42, 46
 – Willet-Holthuysen
 42–43, 46
Museumkaart 6
Museumplein 64
Muziekgebouw aan
 't IJ 54, 92–93
Muziektheater 93
Nationaal Monument 22
 – Vakbondsmuseum
 52, 54
NEMO 53, 54, 57
Nieuwe Kerk 22
 – Spiegelstraat 24, 64
Nieuwmarkt 30
9 Straatjes 25
Noorderkerk 34, 36
Noordermarkt 48
Oosterpark 70
Oost-Indisch Huis 27, 30
Oude Kerk 28
Oudemanhuis Book
 Market 49
Oudemanhuispoort 30
Oudeschans 25
Painting 66–67
Papeneiland 36
Pastoorbrug 36

INDEX

P.C. Hooftstraat 24–25, 64
Pianola Museum 36
Pintohuis 30
Plantenmarkt 49
Portugees Synogoge 44
Prinsengracht 8–9, 33
Queen's Day Market 49
Red Light District 95
Reguliersgracht 46
Rembrandthuis 45, 48
Rembrandtplein 41
Rijksmuseum 58–60, 64
Rotterdam 80–81
Rozengracht 36
Sarphatipark 68, 70
Schreierstoren 29
Shops 72–73, 92
Singel 8, 32
Sint Nicolaaskerk 28–29
Spiegelgracht 25, 64
Stadsschouwburg 93
Stamp and Coin Market 49
Star Ferry Café 39, 54, 88
Stedelijk Museum 62, 64
Stopera 43–44, 46, 93
Studio K 93
't Blauwe Theehuis 64
't Smalle 36, 38
Tassenmuseum Hendrikje 42, 46
Theater Tuschinski 41, 93
The Hague 80
Trippenhuis 30
Tropenmuseum 69, 70
– Junior 57, 69
Tulipomania 35
TunFun 57
Utrecht 76–77
Utrechtsestraat 25
Van Gogh Museum 57, 60, 64
Verzetsmuseum 52
Vondelpark 56, 62, 64
Waag 27–28, 30
Waterlooplein 46, 48
Wertheimpark 54
Westerkerk 34–35
Westermarkt 48
Westerstraat 36
Wijnand Fockinck 39
Woonbootmuseum 35, 36
Zandvoort 76
Zeedijk 30
Zuiderkerk 27, 30

General Editor: Barbara Ender-Jones
Research: Thérèse Van Gelder
Layout: Luc Malherbe, Matias Jolliet
Maps: JPM Publications, Mathieu Germay
Photo credits:
hemis.fr/Borgese p. 4, /Luider p. 51, /Mattes p. 59, /Frilet p. 88, /Maisant p. 96
istockphoto.com/narvikk p. 6, /Evers p. 13 (top), /Ponomarev p. 13 (bottom),
/Robertson pp. 16–17, /Sigler p. 21, /Cattel p. 26, /Price p. 35, /Dixon p. 43, /Jaap2 p. 49,
/Masselink p. 56, /Jezperklauzen p. 61, /jvdwolf p. 77,
/Aardema p. 78, /Kirillov p. 81; wikimedia.org p. 9
Huber/Dutton p. 10, /Kiedrowski p. 33, /Warren p. 90
flickr.com/IISG p. 14, /Godber p. 15, /Milan p. 41, /Paisson p. 53, /Araujo p. 67,
/Triller p. 69, /Saavedra p. 72, /Castellá p. 84, /Cheeseslave p. 87, /Bøtter p. 93
Corbis/Norman p. 18, Serge Olivier pp. 24, 29, 39, 62–63, 95
Travel Pictures Ltd pp. 45, 75, 82; fotolia.com/gandolf p. 76

Copyright © 2012, 1998 JPM Publications S.A., 12, avenue William-Fraisse, 1006 Lausanne, Switzerland
information@jpmguides.com – www.jpmguides.com

All rights reserved. No part of this book may be reproduced or transmitted in any form or by any means, electronic or mechanical, including photocopying, recording or by any information storage and retrieval system without permission in writing from the publisher.

Every care has been taken to verify the information in the guide, but neither the publisher nor his client can accept responsibility for any errors that may have occurred. If you spot an inaccuracy or a serious omission, please let us know.

Printed in Germany – 14879.00.9929 – **Edition 2012**

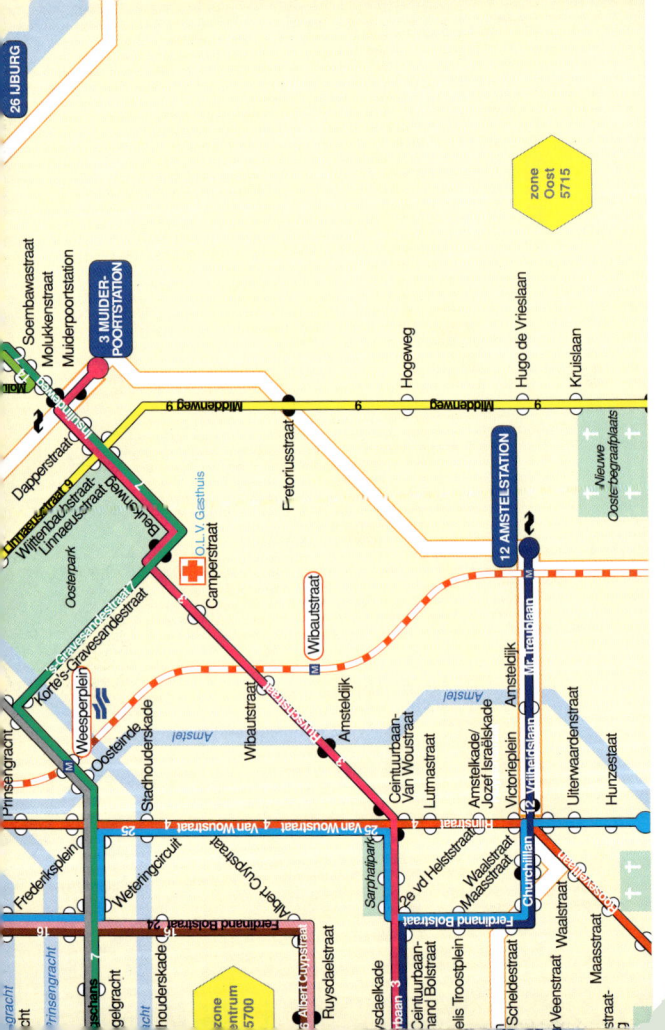